The Angel's Orchestra

A little book that takes you on a big spiritual journey

BY
PATRICIA LADALE LANE

2nd Edition Copyright © 2017 by Patricia LaDale Lane

Published and distributed in the United States by: CreateSpace

All rights reserved. No part of this book may be reproduced by any mechanical, photographic, or electronic process, or in the form of a phonographic recording; nor may it be stored in a retrieval system, transmitted, or otherwise be copied for public or private use – other than for "fair use" as brief quotations embodied in articles and reviews – without prior written permission from the author.

The author of this book does not dispense medical advice or information or prescribe the use of any technique as a form of treatment for any physical, emotional, or medical issues. The intent of the author is to offer general information to assist you in your quest for spiritual well-being. The author assumes no responsibility for actions you take based on information in this book.

Cover Design by James Patrick Lane

Library of Congress Cataloging-in-Publication Data

Lane, Patricia LaDale

The Angel's Orchestra / Patricia LaDale Lane

ISBN 978-1983580277

ISBN-13 1983580279

Published in the United States of America

To Jimmy, Kelly and Sharla

I love you always and eternally…

Contents

Introduction	*i*
Chapter 1 – The Blessings of the Angels	*1*
Chapter 2 – Out of the Mouths of Babes	*5*
Chapter 3 – A Healer in the Family	*11*
Chapter 4 – Dad's Amazing Story	*19*
Chapter 5 – Life Goes On	*23*
Chapter 6 – Phone Call from Spirit	*33*
Chapter 7 – My Own Personal Awakening	*41*
Chapter 8 – The Do Over	*47*
Chapter 9 – Show Me A Sign	*61*
Chapter 10 – Healing the Healer	*67*
Chapter 11 – Archangel Magic	*75*
Chapter 12 – Answering the Call	*93*
Chapter 13 – Working with the Masters	*99*
Chapter 14 – Mediumship	*109*
Chapter 15 – Past Lives and Dying without Regret	*119*
Chapter 16 – Life's Lessons	*127*
Chapter 17 – Conclusion	*141*
Appendix	*145*
How to Read Cards	*145*
The Green Tara Mantra	*153*
A List of Books	*157*
Dedication & Acknowledgements	*161*
About the Author	*163*

Introduction

I have been fortunate in this life. Heaven has opened her gates for me many times and continues to do so. I imagine the gates flinging open and the Angels flying out singing, "It is time! It is time!"

I see all of God's Angels above and around us moving things along, putting people in the right place at the right time and coordinating those chance meetings so we can hear what we are meant to hear at that exact moment we are destined to hear it. Divine timing is a miracle in itself. I don't even begin to understand how it takes place. I believe with every fiber of my being that it happens just as it is written, not by chance, but by God's Grace and our own Divine planning.

If only we were reincarnated each lifetime with the knowledge from our previous lifetimes. Unfortunately, we must relearn what we need to survive on this earth during each incarnation. I do believe many of us come back with a tiny bit of soul remembrance which enables us to recognize feelings, places and a few other souls to a certain degree. And many of us are born with a knowing about some things. For most of us, though, we come back with a clean slate.

I believe that we are Divinely guided each and every moment of our lives whether we realize it or not. Our guides and Angels have knowledge of our past lives and experiences. It is when we realize this fact and learn to trust and to communicate with the unseen that the unseen world, which is beside us all along, can make itself known even more. I picture an orchestra of Angels working to balance, coordinate, and shift all of this guidance behind the scene and just out of sight for our benefit and the benefit of others.

If not for the Angels of Heaven, where do all those magical signs and synchronicities, those urges and sudden inspirations come from? What would the world be if not for this Divine timing and the complex coordination required of those magnificent Messengers of God?

These thoughts and ideas are being put on paper at this very moment because of miraculous occurrences of Divine timing and synchronistic events that have turned my life around. *Realization is the key to understanding.* I have a deep urge inside me to reveal an amazingly simple secret to the world. Nothing is impossible, everything we experience in this life is here for a purpose, and this lifetime was all planned by us before we were born.

I have been led to this perfect place at this perfect time for the opportunity to share the synchronistic miracles that have happened in my life with you so that you may know these things yourself. In this book these miracles have been written with the intent to not only entertain, but to share the magic woven within my life tapestry with a specific purpose in mind for the reader. Within these pages you will find my truths which are a direct result of these experiences.

Hopefully, these stories will inspire you to search for your own truths, to ask your Angels for their assistance, and to recognize the answers they give as the magic of life when they occur. My desire is that you step through any fears you may have so that you may embrace and open your eyes to the possibilities of living the life you dream of and fulfilling your life purpose or, at the very least, to begin that search.

I had always thought I would write a romance novel and this is it! I had thought I would write a book about my life experiences and this is it! I had thought I would write a book to inspire others, spiritually. This is all of those things laid out in simple words from my life experiences and my heart.

So here goes. Grab yourself a cup of tea, settle in and we'll get this show on the road. The only thing you need to keep in mind is that the truth, many times, is stranger than fiction.

Chapter 1

The Blessings of the Angels

Angels are near you. Believe and be open!

When I was a very young child, an Angel would come to me at night after I was tucked into bed, a mere moment before I drifted off to sleep. I remember her vividly - her light was radiant, but not so bright it hurt my eyes as it lit up the dark recesses in the corners of my room and calmed my fears of the darkness and all that lingered there. She was pure white with features beautiful and brilliant in their illumination. She brought with her a gentle energy of peace and protection. With her light next to me, I was able to calmly drop off to sleep while knowing I was safe and being watched over. I would pull the covers over my head to create my little cave made from the blankets, and as soon as I fell asleep I would take flight up into the sanctuary of the clouds in the heavens with my guardian Angel friend.

The Angel's Orchestra

Was my Angel real or was she a figment of my imagination? Did I dream her up while I actually slept? I don't know and I can't say for sure, but I will tell you this, her presence introduced me to the magic of the Angels and since then I continue to talk with them often and turn to them for protection and assistance.

Every night before I drift off to dreamland, I ask the Angels to surround me as I sleep and to protect me and my loved ones. Whenever I get into a car, I ask for my Angels to protect me and watch over others on the road (and how I appreciate those great parking spaces and time warps I receive upon asking when I am in a hurry). When I encounter grief or fear or see ugly things, I ask my Angels to go and comfort those in need and to send those I am praying for a connection to their own Angels. My experiences as a young child taught me to believe in Angels and their abilities. I have always loved Angels and known without a doubt they are real. Angels are a true gift from God sent to assist us and light our way.

As I now read Angel cards and do the intuitive work which I have been clearly guided to do for others, I ask my Angels to be with me and to help me to heal myself and to assist in healing others. When speaking at engagements, I ask them to put the right words in my mouth and give me the courage to stand and talk. I am extremely shy and speaking and teaching require that I continually step through the fears and phobias associated with putting myself out there. Some things worth doing take continual work and speaking in front of others is one of those things for me.

Angels are always there for me and they always have been and I do not doubt they always will be. I cannot imagine a life without Angels and I can't envision a day going by in which I don't talk to them. So, it doesn't matter if I really saw an Angel when I was a child, does it? It doesn't matter if I do or I do not see Angels now or if I never see them with my physical eyes. What matters is the fact that I believe in them and in believing in them I don't really have to see them. I just have faith that they are there. They do not have to prove themselves to me by appearing to me in physical form. They reveal themselves to me in a thousand other ways.

This book is the story of not just one Angel, but an orchestra of Angels. Just as in a symphony orchestra, each Angel plays a special role and possesses unique abilities and powers. God is the orchestra conductor. And, the Angels are his assistants who exist for the sole purpose of helping humans. Angels are present in every religious tradition. They are able to support the needs of an infinite number of people at once, and only have one restriction. They are not permitted to interfere with free will. So, as we seek assistance from the Angels, we must ask them for their help. And, in doing so we bring them happiness and delight for their sole purpose is to serve.

Throughout this journey, I will share with you some of the ways my life has been touched by the Angels and in the end, you can be your own judge whether Angels exist or not. For me, I know they do.

The Angel's Orchestra

Chapter 2

Out of the Mouths of Babes

Children are sensitive to the world of magic and spirit and this awareness should be accepted and encouraged.

When I was a little girl, my Great Grandmother Asbell and Great Aunt Dan (Margaret) lived next door to our little white house in the country. Grandma Asbell was on the maternal side of my family tree and I feel my psychic gifts of seeing and hearing came from her branch of the family - passed down from generation to generation through her Celtic bloodline that traces back to Ireland.

Her daughter, who was my grandmother, possessed magical gifts, and I have heard stories about her seeing leprechauns and fairies dancing on the flat stones down by the creek which ran alongside the back edge of their property.

The Angel's Orchestra

Before going to sleep at night I would roll over to look out the window beside my bed and into the window my grandmother looked out of while she lay in her own bed. Grandma Asbell and I would blow one another kisses through those windows before going to sleep. It was a nightly ritual.

When I was about 5 years old, for several nights, my peaceful sleep was disturbed. I began to have dreams which frightened me—dreams of beautiful flowers and the intensely sweet smells of those flowers accompanied by strange music like I had never heard before. I would awaken in the middle of the night with a fear so intense that it drove me out of my bed to tiptoe quietly on the cold wood floors into my parents' bedroom.

I found comfort sleeping between them and would, most times, awaken in the morning in their bed to find my Dad already off to work and my Mother making me oatmeal for my breakfast. I learned later that these nightmares were actually about funerals. When the dreams began, I had never attended a funeral in my life and the sensations of flowers and unfamiliar music were not recognizable to me in my conscious mind.

One week, I experienced a particularly intense episode of these vivid dreams for several nights in a row. They terrified me so badly that I could not sleep alone, and on one particular morning, when I awoke, I could hear whispering and sensed that an oppressive cloud of sadness had taken over our house. The feelings were so intense that I could barely breathe. My Aunt was there, but my grandmother was not. So, I got dressed and went to look for her.

In the early hours of the morning, Grandma was most likely to be found in the little garden behind her red stone cottage dressed in her black bonnet and one of the long, dark prairie dresses she often wore. She loved working in the cool of the morning before the hot Texas sun reached its peak, chasing rabbits out of her green beans or removing the huge, poisonous copperhead snakes that were a constant threat to country living in Texas. Her reliable old hoe that we children were not allowed to touch was always in her hand when we were in the garden, both as a razor-edged weeding tool and a protective weapon.

It was still early in the morning before the Texas sun arose overhead and made the heat intolerable and too uncomfortable to be outside. At this time of day, Grandma should be in our garden, and it was customary for me to bring her a dipper of cool water from the big aluminum pail she filled each morning from the hand pump next to her big, deep farmhouse sink.

Sometimes, when I arrived early enough, Grandma would sit me on the countertop and let me pump the bucket full of fresh water and help her carry it to the garden to water our plants. Later in the day we would shuck the peas we had harvested earlier or snap the green beans and clean the carrots and the onions. On this particular morning, I was surprised to discover that Grandma was not to be found in the garden and the bucket on her kitchen counter was dry.

It turned out that my dreams of the previous night had in fact, been a premonition. I was told that Grandma had gone to live with the Angels during the night. I could not understand this as we had just blown one another good night kisses before falling asleep. Where was she?

Looking back, I realize how very old and frail she had become. When I thought of Grandma, the things I missed most was seeing her at night before I went to sleep and sitting on the porch steps while she read children's Bible stories to me and my little sister, Allee.

I recall so vividly when I realized what had been happening. I was standing between my mom and my dad at Grandma Asbell's funeral and looking at that beautiful pink gown she was dressed in. I reached up and pulled on my mom's shirt and whispered that I knew this place as I had seen my Grandma in that dress - looking like an Angel. This was exactly the same scene that had been replaying over and over as I slept. The nightly visions of the flowers and their sickly sweet smell made me ill. I had experienced this moment before – in my dreams.

I saw the surprise on my mother's face that she quickly tried to conceal - along with a tiny gasp when I told her this was what had been waking me up and scaring me so badly. She became very pale, and I remember to this day that a *look* passed between her and my father. You know the *look* I am talking about. It was the same one they got on their faces when I did something they did not approve of. When I saw that look at Grandma's funeral, I knew that I had done something very wrong, but did not know what it was.

When my parents realized that my nightmares had actually been premonitions of someone's passing, they made the decision that I was not to be permitted to attend any more funerals. This stigma around funerals caused me to be afraid of death. I didn't understand what it was about me and why I didn't get to say goodbye to so many family members including my dad's father or my Uncle Bill - for whom I still carry regret. My cousins were all at those funerals and I recall feeling so left out and not understanding why I was not allowed to go. It wasn't until several decades later that I understood why.

A few years ago I was having a conversation with one of my older cousins and she said that everyone in the family knew I predicted deaths. But, I didn't, I just dreamt about them! In fact, I had almost completely forgotten about the dreams I had just before my grandmother's death until I was reminded of it during that same casual conversation with this cousin I had not seen since I was a child. It all came flooding back. The memory of the dreams had eluded me and shifted into the far recesses of my mind. Those memories were suddenly brought back when my cousin said, "You used to dream of being at someone's funeral and then they would die so that's why you weren't allowed to go to funerals. It was creepy."

I then recalled those memories of crawling into my parents' bed and even remembered my visions of the Angel who came to me at night.

The next funeral I went to after Grandma's was when I was eighteen years old and one of my schoolmates was killed in an automobile accident the summer of my senior year. This was a boy I had dated, and it was a big loss to me. I do not recall having dreams of his passing, however. I feel that my Angels blocked these recollections in order to protect me.

I believe the reason I chose to forget those types of dreams was because I felt I had done something wrong and caused my grandmother's death. Why else would I be punished and not allowed to attend another funeral until adulthood? I felt guilty for the first time in my life. My parents didn't want me to talk about seeing the Angel in my room at night because it scared them. The memories of my dreams began to quickly fade and to this day, I believe it is one of the reasons I have difficulty recalling my dreams.

Chapter 3

A Healer in the Family

We choose our parents to help fulfill
our soul purpose.

Our souls choose our parents, our gender, our siblings, our nationalities – so that we can learn the lessons we need to learn in each lifetime. My dad, in particular, had a profound impact on my spiritual development both through our shared ancestors and life experiences.

My father's ancestry was mostly Native American, and as a result, he was a beautiful man with dark brown skin, chiseled facial features, and brilliant green eyes. I am blessed to have my father's eyes. His skin would take on a reddish hue when he was in the sun, and he often worked outside because he was a carpenter by trade. On many occasions, my girlfriends would remark about how handsome my dad was.

My dad's family has mental illness running rampant; bipolar disorder, depression and anxiety combined with many years of dependency on drugs and alcohol have taken over the lives of many of the members of his side of my family. I know there is deep sensitivity to energy on Dad's side, and many of these illnesses are probably the result of that. As empaths, my relatives simply *feel* more deeply than other people and since they have challenges processing all of those feelings and emotions - they medicate to cope.

I share in the empathic ability that has been passed on through my father's lineage – and I consider this same sensitivity to the feelings of others to be a precious gift.

Fortunately, I was able to break my family's cycle of substance abuse in my own life. I was a teenager in the early 1970's and exposed to drugs and alcohol during my high school years. I confess that I experimented with alcohol and marijuana in my later teenage years like most of my friends, and yet, something held me back from going overboard.

I believe the reason I made the decision to avoid becoming addicted like most of my family was due to several things. First of all, I observed my dad's alcoholism and how it affected our quality of life. I have always needed peace, and there was little peace in my childhood with the fighting and misery that is part of living with an alcoholic family member. Secondly, I did not like the feeling of not being in control of myself and my own body. Finally, I believe that my Angels guided me to find my solace in other things such as reading and dreaming of making a better life for myself. I envisioned having a good career and the stability and security I would feel when I was an adult. Financial stability and all that went with it was very important to me after growing up in a household that struggled and I began to work at the young age of 15 in order to get the things I wanted and to not be a financial burden to my family.

I know that my interest in energy work and my innate desire to help others was passed down from my dad's Native American roots, because like many Native Americans, I can actually feel the pain and suffering of the people I meet. And, as many people who are called to heal others, my greatest lessons about life and death and serving as a healer came from supporting my dad on his healing journey.

When I was in my mid-thirties, I was called to help my father, who was battling severe COPD (Chronic Obsessive Pulmonary Disorder), a disease that interferes with lung function and makes it difficult to breathe. Dad had suffered for years and had been hospitalized many times and experienced several close calls. I had been with him before during his hospital stays and, as the oldest child, my parents placed their faith in me and relied on me. After arriving at the hospital, I was able to give the medical staff the information they needed concerning medicines, allergies, doctors and past hospital stays. Even though I felt deeply concerned for my dad, during times of crisis, it was almost as if another person took over my body so I could provide the strength and support that was needed.

However, this time was different than before and my dad's condition quickly escalated to become the most difficult hospital visit yet. Dad's condition did not improve after being pumped with the medicines that usually opened up his lung capacity. There seemed to be no relief in sight as he sat on the side of the ER bed and leaned over the small side table which supported his weight.

I did what I had always done, acting as my dad's breath coach. I recall saying, "Now, breathe deep into your belly and let your stomach swell. Imagine the oxygen going through your veins. That's it, breathe in and breathe out slowly and focus on your breath and don't panic. It's going to be OK."

Only it wasn't going to be OK - my dad simply could not breathe and the medicine wasn't able to work its magic quickly enough. His skin color was slowly becoming darker, and I knew this was a bad sign. I could see the pain he was experiencing radiating through those beautiful green eyes, wordlessly pleading with me to do something. I felt totally helpless.

My mother kept repeating, "Virgil! Virgil!" getting louder with each syllable and more panicked each time she said his name. This is it - I thought to myself. This is the place and the time he will die. I will remember this moment for the rest of my life. He is so young and this is not fair. What are we going to do without him? What is my Mom going to do and how will she manage after losing her soulmate?

When Dad did not have the strength to hold his head up any longer, he quietly laid his head down on the aluminum hospital tray and simply stopped breathing. Instantly, the doctors and nurses shoved my mother and me out of the room as they ran in while rolling huge pieces of medical equipment with them. This was all happening so fast, and suddenly my mother and I found ourselves in the hall looking at one another in shock on the other side of a closed door, and not remembering how we got there. We knew our beloved was gone and could not believe what had just happened. I could see the disbelief on my mom's face and feel her shock in the pit of my stomach. She looked so frail and so old having spent the last ten years caring for a sick man and working a full time job to help support them.

My heart was pounding and body was shaking, but I felt like I had to do something. I told Mom to stay where she was in case the doctors came out looking for someone. I motioned for her to sit on the bench outside the door and told her I would go to the waiting room and let my siblings know what had just happened.

Although I did not know this immediately, my beautiful father with a heart of gold had actually died and crossed over to the other side for a short period of time. He actually had a Near Death Experience (NDE). In a last minute attempt to save his life, he was resuscitated and placed on a ventilator, a huge piece of medical equipment that took over breathing for my dad when he no longer had the strength to breathe for himself. We learned later that the reason for Dad's weakened condition and the fact that the drugs weren't effective as they had been before was that Dad was also suffering from pneumonia.

I can only imagine how frightening it was for him to awaken the next morning hooked up to this intimidating machine. When I first saw Dad after he awoke from sedation, he looked confused and weak and tired and a bit angry. It was apparent he wanted to talk, but was not able to do that because of the tubes running into his mouth and down into his lungs. We knew he did not want to be hooked up to this machine. We knew he was upset; however it would be weeks later before he would be able to explain why he was so frustrated. He remained in the hospital for 18 days in order to give his body the time it needed to respond to the antibiotics and regain his strength again.

During this stressful time, my mind was racing and I was questioning everything – past, present and future. I wondered if it would have been better for him if we had let him go, because the inevitable was still looming in front of us. He was going to die. There was no cure for this disease. He had no hope for a normal life and no hope of getting well. Was he to become bedridden and on oxygen the remainder of his days? Why-oh-why did the doctors do this to him? Now, he was going to have to suffer more in order to die all over again. It just did not make any sense to me, for someone to have to go through the process of dying a second time.

I knew Dad realized all of this and yet, when I looked into his eyes, I expected to see the fear I had seen only a few short hours before – but it was not there. Where had that fear gone? Was he just too exhausted to be afraid? What had changed in my father? No one in the hospital had asked us if this is what we wanted for him. Surely, we would have told them no! We had talked about all of this before as a family hadn't we? We should have. Now, it was too late and we had to deal with this all over again and probably very soon. What could possibly be the purpose of this decision the doctors had made?

Things eventually calmed down and we were able to talk with Dad's doctors. We learned that his pulmonary doctor had made the decision to put him on the ventilator in anticipation that Dad would be strong enough to be taken off of it once the pneumonia was given time to respond to the antibiotics.

When Dad finally came home after spending three weeks in the hospital, he was pale and very weak and he was not able to go anywhere without oxygen. He returned home a very different man from the one he had been before the NDE and the changes were not all physical. The fear of death that he had dealt with for so long had disappeared and I could see the new sense of calm in his eyes. He had a secret that he would be sharing with us soon. He had been given a glimpse of Heaven and our world would never look quite the same to him. My dad had been given a wondrous gift. He had seen the other side and he knew it was really something to look forward to. He was no longer afraid and he wanted to go back. He could hardly wait to share his story.

The Angel's Orchestra

Chapter 4

Dad's Amazing Story

Magic is everywhere. Be open to it!

Dad shared with us that when he first felt himself leave his body, it was very sudden and then, there he was, up on the ceiling of the room looking down as the medical staff swarmed around his body in their accelerated task to save his life. He said he barely recognized himself as belonging to that body lying lifelessly on that hospital bed. It didn't feel like he was in that body. He said that he could sense what each of the medical staff was thinking and feeling all at the same time, he was actually experiencing their emotions as he looked at them, curious about what they were doing because he felt no connection to the body lying there.

Then, my dad was there with my mother and me on the other side of the door where we had found ourselves sitting on that bench. He focused his attention on my mother and the love he had for her at that moment. The love he had for her was all encompassing. He was conscious of what was going on in the room where his body was and simultaneously aware of me when I left to speak with my siblings and he recalled witnessing their reactions and what they said when I told them, "I think our father has passed away." He later recited this sentence word-for-word back to us.

While he was there in that emergency waiting room with us, he saw some kind of tunnel open up above him and he felt pulled like a magnet and began to slowly move closer to it. He could see a brilliant light at the end of the long tunnel. He felt the urge to go inside of it as the light pulled him forward like a magnet. He was not aware of any other souls around him or in the tunnel. He did see shadows in the light at the end of the tunnel as he made his way up towards the light and into the tunnel itself. He sensed the shadows were waiting there for him. Whatever and whoever these shadows were - he did not know. He could feel the love radiating out of the light and he wanted to go to that light. He was not afraid and felt like he was going home. This feeling of love and familiarity is what he said he could not describe in words and that sensation is what he remembered most.

While all of this was happening, he said that he heard the most beautiful sounds all around him and he called it music except it was unlike any music he had ever heard. "The Angels were singing to me and they were singing music I had never heard before in the most beautiful voices I have ever heard. It was my music and my sound, and it was being played for me."

My dad felt the presence of the Angels and did not hesitate to assure us it was the Angels who were playing the music. Somehow he just knew. Of all these things, the one thing that my father mentioned with the most emphasis was the feeling of peace that came over him. He had no regrets, no sadness, no guilt, no anxiety, and no pain. He recalled only a feeling of peace and love, of being cherished, and his overwhelming desire to go to this light.

He almost made it.

Suddenly, he was pulled back into that weak and broken body and awoke shortly afterwards to find himself dependent on a machine to sustain his earthly life. Dad's disappointment at being brought back was apparent as he asked me shortly after he was able to speak and even before he told us about the NDE, "Why did you let them bring me back?" At the time, he was disappointed and very weak and tired. Eventually, though, I believe he came to realize that he was supposed to tell others about his experience and that there was a great purpose for his remaining days.

I believe he was brought back because there were some things which have been a direct result of his coming back that needed to happen before he finally departed the Earth plane. He had important work to finish and needed to remain here - if only for a short time longer.

Dad's NDE turned out to be a gift not only to him, but to me and over time, it transformed my own journey. When my father lost his fear of death, deep inside of myself, I wanted that feeling, too! Imagine living without the fear of dying. How freeing would that be? How would letting go of fear change my life? Tremendously, because at that time, I had a horrible fear of everything, not enough money, not smart enough, what if something happened to me and I could not work and support my children or what if something happened to one of my children? At that time, I lived in a world of fear, a world of my own creation.

Chapter 5

Life Goes On

*We are all here to learn lessons and
the obstacles we face in life are
the greatest teachers.*

I woke up in the morning with fear and I went to sleep after tossing and turning for hours on end with those same fears. If I didn't have something to worry about, I would make something up. I was a single mother, and an emotional mess and I constantly fed that monster of fear.

So here goes, I must tell you the things which are not so pretty in my life in order to get to all the good stuff - the lessons I've learned by working through trials and tribulations. This is the core reason I am putting forth the effort to write this all down. I don't tell this tale for pity or sympathy, but my hope is that these incidents and the wisdom I now embrace with all of my heart and soul, will give you new perspective as you move forward on your own journey.

We must realize that life is like a play and we are all here in our assigned roles to assist on this journey. The parts we play were assigned to us a long time ago and how far we go and what we learn and what we experience in order to share and grow is up to us. The biggest part of this equation is simply to let go of the things which hold us back and to realize this one thing. We are all on this journey together and we are all equal in the eyes of the Divine and we are all here to experience all that our lives have to offer.

At the time of my father's NDE, I had gone through a horrendous divorce from my first husband leaving me in shock and completely broken mentally, emotionally, and financially. I was struggling to raise my two young daughters with very little income from a job as a bank teller. I felt stuck because banks are notorious for offering low wages and for frequent layoffs and this knowledge added to my stress and fear.

And, my living situation didn't help me feel better about anything. Although I hated the neighborhood where I lived and the old house I rented after the divorce - it was all I could afford at the time. I also needed to be close to my parents, to my job, and to my kids' school.

My mother often watched my two girls for me in the evenings because I was working long, hard hours to support my children. We lived on a wage that did not stretch very far and I paid half of what I made in daycare. We were really struggling to make ends meet. I was trying to remain optimistic after experiencing my world falling apart overnight only a few months earlier. It was a one day at a time existence, and I felt like I was broken into little pieces - and the light from my heart and spirit was extremely dim.

I was overwhelmed with anger and regret. I was angry at my husband. He betrayed me in the worst ways imaginable by falling in love with my best friend and getting her pregnant. I was angry at him for abandoning me and our children. I was angry at myself because I had not gotten a better education so I could be more independent and self-sufficient. I regretted that I had not saved enough money to help me get through this situation. I was angry that I had lost my beautiful home and had to live in the old house in the old neighborhood with the rats and the roaches. I was angry because I worked all the time and spent so much time away from my children and still could not afford to buy them the food and the clothes they needed. I had no savings and I felt I was being punished for something I could not figure out. I was bitter and mad at myself and the world and I was afraid. I was very afraid.

Everything I had worked for the past twelve years was gone, and I had nothing to show for it. What had all that hard work been for? I had supported my ex-husband when he lost his job, and what had I received in return? Abandonment and humiliation, that's what! I felt like I had been cast away like an old pair of shoes. I was embarrassed that he had walked away from me and our family and felt like others were laughing at me. I was humiliated that I had not been smart enough to know what was going on behind my back.

I felt stupid and numb and betrayed and used by two of the people I had trusted and loved most in the world.

How could I ever learn to trust again? How would I ever love again? How could I ever have fun again? How could I ever feel safe and secure again? Humpty Dumpty had fallen off the wall and there were no King's men around to help me put the pieces back together again. My life had become one big pity party. I felt as low as a person can feel and I couldn't envision a way out.

This wasn't how I had planned my life.

The list of "what ifs, hows and whys" went on and on and on, but you get the picture. I hated my ex-husband and I hated my ex-girlfriend and I hated the situation they had created. I had been so stupid in my choices. If the truth be told, I hated myself and this self-hatred festered like a disease for many, many years. I was caught up in a world of bitterness and distrust and hate and began looking for love in all the wrong places.

I refused to take any responsibility for the breakup and honestly, I had known for many years that there was something missing in that marriage because we had not been happy for a long time. I knew almost immediately after marrying my husband that I had made a mistake. I did love him in my own way and I loved our children very much but, we were not a good match and had never been a good match.

We had nothing in common - and most of that time was spent doing things that he liked to do and I cared little about such as camping and partying and drinking and playing card games. I began to lose myself in that marriage, but I did not realize it at the time. I wore the rose colored glasses and never took them off until the day my husband came home from work, packed his bags, and walked out the door with me on my hands and knees begging him not to go. Not a pretty picture, but a real one.

I had always been more of a loner enjoying time spent with myself and a good book or music while he surrounded himself with friends and had parties every weekend. After our children were born, I did not have the energy for all of this extracurricular activity. It was all I could manage to work all week, to take care of the house and the two babies and cook the meals and pay the bills. You get the picture. I gave and gave and did not receive very much in return.

My greatest desire at the end of the day, after the girls were in bed was to crawl into bed by myself with a good book and put ear plugs in my ears to drown out the noise of the drinking and partying going on in the other rooms of the house. To outsiders, our marriage looked good. We had new cars and a beautiful home. But, in reality our life together was a sham. We rarely talked to one another and had lots of debt. Trying to keep up with the Joneses was expensive and exhausting.

I felt unfulfilled and could not figure out why this was happening. What had been missing? Looking back I can clearly see that he was not the man I was meant to marry. It is so clear to look back and see this. I had sold myself short, and to make matters worse, I had left someone else behind and broken his heart in order to marry the man I thought would be best able to support me and a family at that time.

Sadly, I didn't learn from my mistakes with my first husband and married again to escape the struggles of trying to survive on my own. I hadn't learned to love and respect myself and I also didn't listen to my intuition.

I married my second husband, and although I cared about him - we were so very different and I knew it from the start. I heard in my mind and even felt in my gut that I was making another mistake. I heard that little voice say no! no! no! even louder than before. I just knew from the start something was not right and felt wrong. I jumped into this situation to quell my fears of being alone and to ease the financial stress I was under.

This marriage became extremely difficult within a year and in hindsight, I should have left after the signs appeared that this relationship was wrong in so many ways. After the first divorce from my children's father, I was determined that my second marriage would survive come hell or high water. As a result, I stayed in the hell way too long because of the fear of being a single parent again and because I did not want to face failure and be marked as a two time loser.

I quickly realized I had married the second time mostly for security. What I ended up with was a marriage that was so turbulent that my children dreaded being in the same house with me and my husband, let alone in the same room. My daughters could not wait until they graduated from high school to leave the mess in which they had been raised. All they remember are the arguments. To be honest, that is what I remember mostly also - the fighting. It is difficult when I think about it to even acknowledge all of the complicated dynamics of that marriage and the reasons it was not a safe place for me or for my two girls. Being married to this man was like trying to blend oil and water, but I was determined to make the situation work. However, no matter what I did, the marriage just got worse.

I left a few times only to have him come and talk me into going back again. I began to realize that if I left, he would keep coming after me because he had become so dependent on me for the simplest things and he loved me in his own way. Sadly, his affection for me contributed to his jealous and controlling personality and that pushed me even further away. I became an angry person and lashed out at his constant criticism and was always on the defensive.

This was an unhealthy, co-dependent relationship - and I was the loser. I spent over twenty years in that marriage and unfortunately, by the time I decided to leave, it literally took everything I had – including my physical health. Looking back, I believe I was actually dying. I did not honor and love myself, and so I gave all of my life force away.

For lack of a better description - energetically, I was being drained and he was the one doing the draining. I did not understand energies and how to protect mine, and I became totally depleted. Our energy is our life force and I gave away my life force, willingly and unknowingly.

It wore me down to the point in which I became extremely depressed, and it is painful to share with you that I was not even sure if I wanted to live during the last few years of that marriage. It was not all my ex-husband's fault. We are both to blame. We just approached the world from different perspectives and we disagreed about so many things. As I look back, I realize that he could not help being who and what he was any more than I could have changed myself or what I believed in.

When my youngest went off to college, I began to work longer and longer hours. I had a very stressful job and overtime was part of the bargain. I began to work some ridiculously long hours as a means of escape. Let's face it, I did not want to be in the energy at home and I had no sacred space to call my own.

Towards the end of the marriage, I began to dream of ways to leave. I kept many of my things packed in boxes, dreaming of a quick escape. I shopped a lot and bought things I did not need to fill the empty spaces inside me and take up my time. But, eventually I realized that all the stuff I bought could not fill those empty places inside of me.

I knew the house was his and that everything inside the house was his as well. He told me that so often that I believed it. When I left, I gave him everything because I did not love myself enough to fight for what legally belonged to me and he kept everything - including the wedding ring he had bought me, the dishes my mother had given me for Christmas, and the house we had purchased together.

I almost completely lost myself in that relationship, and that scares me the most. I am a very different person today than I was back then. As human beings, we are constantly changing and evolving and I am so grateful that I had the courage to finally leave that marriage for good.

I am sharing these personal experiences because I want to help others who are suffering through similar situations to view their lives not as victims but, instead, as people who are able to take charge of their lives and to control their own destinies. I want others to see purpose in their lives and to realize why they are experiencing challenges that can feel overwhelming at the time.

What if these are instead gifts to accelerate our learning and in doing so to evolve our souls? What if we plan all of these events ourselves at soul level? I believe we do. When we choose to incarnate in human form, we choose these experiences and we choose the souls who will be a part of our lessons.

When our lifetimes are over, we will realize at a soul level that those who hurt us the most are the ones who are in service to us. Some of those who mistreat us are actually here to help us.

Each and every challenge we face and overcome in life has the potential to help us learn the major lessons we chose to benefit from in this lifetime. When we share our stories and wisdom from a place of love and understanding, our experiences have the potential to help others who are facing similar challenges in their lives.

So, what did I learn from my second marriage? What nuggets of wisdom do I wish to share with you? First, learn about energy and about how to protect your energies. Learn to hear and listen to that voice inside when it says no, and learn to trust that gut feeling. And, learn how to love and value yourself. These are just some of the things that life experience taught me. The other thing I have learned is that sometimes, mysteries happen that don't seem to have logical explanations.

The Angel's Orchestra

Chapter 6

Phone Call from Spirit

Sometimes unexplainable things happen - through the magic of Divine intervention.

Sometimes things happen – mysteries of life that we can't explain. We just have no option but to believe and have faith. The story I'm about to share is one of those mysteries and I believe that this message my dad received and his being alive to share it with us is also one of the reasons why he returned to us after the NDE.

Dad had been home from the hospital for about 3 months when I went to visit my parents one Saturday morning. I visited often because I had rented a home across the street after my recent divorce from my first husband.

As I walked in the front door of my parents' small home, I smelled Jimmy Dean sausage and bacon frying in the old cast iron skillet along with the scents of biscuits in the oven. I knew there would be gravy soon because this was my dad's favorite breakfast. The grape jelly was on the counter alongside the butter and it was almost time to eat. As I walked into the tiny bedroom to give Dad a hug, I heard the sound of plates clinking as Mom pulled them out of the cabinet and placed them on the counter.

I bent down to kiss Dad on the cheek and noticed he had been crying and asked, "Is something wrong? Are you not feeling well this morning?" He looked at me with a strange expression in his eyes as if he had been deep in thought and answered, "I'll let your Mom tell you about it. I'll be in the kitchen in a minute."

My dad's morning routine was to wake up and immediately do a breathing treatment and use his inhalers. As soon as he ate something, he took a handful of pills. Dad needed oxygen full time now and had to contend with several cumbersome tubes. He lost a lot of weight during his hospital stay and appeared frail. He no longer radiated the vibrancy he had when he was younger and healthier. He would never gain back the weight or reclaim the beautiful color to his skin. What had once been the simple task of breathing now consumed too much of his energy. Dad had always been a tall, lanky man. In fact his nickname had been "Slim." But, nonetheless, before he fought COPD, he was never considered skinny.

I turned from him and replied, "Take your time, Daddy, see you in the kitchen in a few minutes. Your breakfast sure does smell good."

In the kitchen, I found my Mom working hard and looking at her, I immediately saw she had been crying, as well. Thoughts of a relative passing away immediately crossed my mind and I started running down the long list of cousins, aunts and uncles who were mostly living far away from us wondering who it was this time.

"Mom, what's wrong?" I asked.

Looking me in the eye she shocked me by saying, "I am not sure whether to tell you this or not, because I am still in shock and I am not really sure of this myself. I am still trying to figure it out and to understand what happened. I don't want you to think your dad and I are going crazy."

Unexpectedly taken back with surprise by these words, I gently probed, "Mom, tell me. You know I would never think such a thing. I know you and Dad better than that."

My mother had never hidden things from me and my three siblings. She was an open book, and I inherited that trait from her. Furthermore, she knew I never would have questioned or judged or considered my parents to be crazy. I knew my parents were truthful and that they did not make things up. They were two of the most honest and ethical people I ever knew. Whatever motivated my mom to make a statement like this concerned me - to say the least.

I heard my dad call from the bedroom in his weak voice, "Tell her, Leta. We need to talk to someone about this and we need to see what Pattie thinks about what happened last night."

I promptly sat down at the countertop and looked my Mother in the eye. "OK, Mom, what has happened? I need to know. You guys are sort of scaring me."

As my mother began to talk she kept her hands busy plating the breakfast for my dad who was just now slowly walking into the room looking so very tired with his swollen eyes and his shallow cheeks and his inability to take a normal breath.

"It was about 2:30 when the phone rang and I jumped out of bed to answer it." she began, "On the other end of the line, there was a voice that sounded just like John Brown."

John B was one of Dad's best friends. They had both suffered from COPD for many years having been carpenters and breathing in the sawdust from that trade all their lives. They saw the same doctor and even shared their medicines with one another when the need arose.

John did not have much money and survived on disability from social security as my dad did. They did what they could for one another and they had a close bond because they both knew they were very ill. I had not seen John in years but dad talked to him often. I was puzzled by the look on my mom's face because there wasn't anything that strange about John calling them except that it was in the middle of the night.

Mom continued, "This voice that sounded exactly like John B said all happy and carefree - Well, hello, Leta Lee Lane. It is good to hear your voice." Mom paused for a minute looking intently at me as I raised my eyebrow and cocked my head in anticipation of what she would say next. She continued, "I asked - Who is this? And he just laughed and answered - now you know who this is, never stating his name."

After a short pause Mom said the voice on the other end of the phone then asked if Virgil was there and she answered, "Yes." To which he replied, "No need to get him up out of the bed, just tell him that everything is juuuussst fine." just like that, long and drawn out. And then the voice began to laugh just like John and still laughing he said, "OH! I am going to get in trouble for this one. I have to go now!" There was another laugh and at that point the phone went dead.

Puzzled, I looked at Mom and Dad. "So, what was so unusual about all of this besides that he sounded good when he hasn't in years and he woke you two up?"

Mom looked me straight in the eye and replied, "Pattie, John has been dead for three weeks."

Stunned, I responded to that remark, "What! Then that wasn't John on the phone, who was it and why would someone play a prank like that?"

Mom looked at me and said, "It was John. I know his voice well enough and he is the only one who ever called me Leta Lee Lane like that. I am telling you, it was John Brown."

"Mom, it couldn't have been *him*, maybe you just dreamed it."

My dad, who was sitting next to me by now, said in a serious voice, "Then, you tell me how we both had the very same dream and neither one of us has gone back to sleep. Just like your Mom said, it was not a dream. It happened and we both are here wide awake talking about the same phone call."

"Well, I can't explain it," I answered, only now beginning to realize the implications of what my parents were saying.

Dad continued, "John and I knew we were dying, and soon. We just did not know which one of us would go the soonest so we made a pact. If I died first, I would try to contact him someway and if he died first, he would try to contact me. We made a pact and that was John B carrying through with what he promised he would try to do."

OK, so there it is in a nutshell—this phone call from the grave. This was a life changing event for me and for my parents. The fact that this was a shared experience by both Mom and Dad causes this incident to stand out from many of the other stories I have discovered about similar experiences. Often these events involve only one person having the experience. In my parents' case, they both were involved, first hand. This is extremely powerful for me and for others with whom I have shared this story.

I do not believe that people make these stories up. I know my parents didn't. This phone call from John happened to them together and they were courageous enough to share it with me and with my siblings, their friends and family, despite the fact that the event brought up memories and emotions of pain and loss.

While I cannot explain when and why these things occur to only a select few people, I believe that these remarkable things happen to those who are more open to experiencing something of this nature. Because of my dad's NDE, I believe that a doorway was opened that shifted his energetic vibration and he may have brought back a piece of his higher self to this plane—that by experiencing the miracle of the NDE, he was more open to this incident. I just don't know, but I do know without a doubt that this event actually happened. I know John was able to somehow break through the veil to communicate with my parents through a phone call three weeks after he died.

The Angel's Orchestra

Chapter 7

My Own Personal Awakening

Divine timing leads to Divine lessons.

My dad's NDE lit that spark of desire inside of me to learn more about his experience and what others had to say with similar stories. Because of the changes I saw in him - and what he had felt and seen in those few sacred moments I was thirsty for knowledge.

My research led me to discover that these things do happen. In fact, they occur in more people's lives than any of us realize. Not in everyone's life, but mystical appearances and unexplainable spiritual events do take place more often than we are aware.

Dad's near death experience is just one of those instances of Divine timing I mentioned earlier in this book. It was this event that led me in a new direction in my spiritual journey. It not only changed my perspective about life and death, but it caused me to shift my perspective about spirituality and interaction with the Divine. It was like the veil had been parted a little wider and, maybe just maybe, I was being given guidance to explore even more of the unknown.

Dad's NDE motivated me to read every book I could get my hands on to learn more. Raymond Moody, Bettie J. Eadie, and Dannion Brinkley had all written about their NDE's and the extraordinary experiences of other near death survivors. It was the early eighties and I was thirsty to find the answers! All of these books I was reading would eventually lead me to others as I searched and attempted to quench my thirst for the answers to my questions, and in the process opening my arms wide to embrace all that I could on the subject of near death experiences.

I was constantly amazed by the number of friends and acquaintances who did not know about, and had never heard of a near death experience. I was disappointed by the ones who did not believe even after all of the evidence. I was on fire and was being led to learn as much as possible. As my knowledge expanded, I wanted to understand more about why we humans go through the things we do. What are we here to learn? What is our purpose? What does it all mean? Do we really reincarnate? Have we been here before? Why had I not heard of this before? Why did it resonate so deeply with me?

When I ran across something in my research that did not feel comfortable or that frightened me, I would set it aside or throw it away. I discarded many books in those early years of research, not because I was steeped in the dogma of a traditional Christian upbringing, but because they simply did not resonate as true to me.

I consider myself fortunate because besides a few memories of Bible school and Baptist church services with my dad's mother, Grandma Lane, I had not been bought up with the filters developed by most people who are raised in a traditional Church. I was like a free bird to explore everything I could get my hands on with nothing but my own intuition guiding me.

Looking back, I realize that I did not need a church to find God. I have always been connected, as we all are, and I have always prayed and talked to God directly. When I see something that a particular religion imposes upon its members that does not resonate, I will often think or say out loud, "That is not the God I believe in."

While truth exists in all religious traditions, man's interpretation of that truth is a factor, as well, and it is in *our interpretation* where our own personal truths unfold. I believe that we can feel in our souls when something is true and something is not true. It is a filter we each have in our hearts - this knowing whether something is right or it is wrong, and it resides right there next to that spark of life force energy we each have that is connected to our Creator.

As I continued to read and learn, I realized that we are spiritual beings having a human experience. We are souls inhabiting bodies. Our souls incarnated initially in an unknown process designed by the Creator. I believe that our souls choose when and how to be born as humans and determine the themes of our life paths and lessons. I also believe that, according to Divine timing, when the soul is ready to return to the other side, the soul chooses and there is nothing any human interaction can do to change that timing.

If we have faith, then we must believe in Divine timing for the two go hand in hand. Just know and believe that there is Divine timing in every event, in every meeting, and in everything that we encounter in this world.

Divine timing is one of the most precious gifts we are given and the way it is orchestrated is beyond my comprehension. I don't know or understand how it works, but I do know it exists and in knowing this, I have been able to put aside many of my regrets about the past and my anxieties about the future and to learn to trust in this unseeable and untouchable piece of the puzzle. On the day that my father returned to be with his Maker, I was once again challenged to move forward with love and acceptance.

Approximately a year after his NDE and after receiving the phone call from John Brown, Dad returned to the hospital for his final dance with life. This time, my family and I knew and were forced to accept that fact that he was dying. When Dad checked in to the hospital, his favorite doctor was on vacation. Dad loved this doctor and this doctor loved my dad. Upon returning from his trip, the doctor came to check on Dad, and looked surprised to see his weakened condition when he came into the room.

My dad barely had the energy to speak, so the doctor bent down to his ear and whispered, "Virgil, is there anything I can do for you?" to which my dad, barely conscious, whispered, "I hurt."

This humanitarian Doctor placed his hand on Dad's heart and said "I promise you, Virgil, I am going to take care of that and you will not hurt anymore." Almost immediately, a nurse appeared with a needle, gave my father an injection and he lost consciousness a moment later.

He never regained it, and passed away peacefully within a few hours. On the morning of his final day, Dad told us he saw four Angels in the room, one in each corner. With their special escort, I have no doubt he crossed over in an experience filled with peace and grandeur.

I feel compelled to say two things about the process of returning to the other side, and the decisions we and our loved ones face when the end is nearing. It takes courage to know what is right and to do the right thing. And, if life loses its value, then why should people fight to prolong a person's life and extend the suffering? We will all face death someday and we need not fear death even though our Western society traditionally teaches us to fight it and dread it with all of our might. Death is merely a shift of our energy as humans. Our soul leaves the body and lives on. And, it does so according to the mystery of Divine timing.

When my time comes - I want to go without struggle and not have this life prolonged when it is no longer valuable. And, I want to come back again, as soon as possible because I love this playground we call Earth.

The Angel's Orchestra

Chapter 8

The Do Over

It's never too late for true love to
walk through the door...

Studying about near death experiences opened the door for me to begin to yearn to learn everything I could about spirituality and my own purpose. Some things seem to be unexplainable, but it is when we actually begin to encounter these events personally that it all begins to make sense. The more I studied, the more I began to notice different synchronicities happening in my life. I also began to listen to my intuition. It helped me to let go of fear, have faith, and, as a result, a new paradigm was being created and things gradually began to change and improve.

And that is the purpose of this book, to share what I know, what I have experienced with each and every one of you so that wherever you are in your journey, you can leave the fear behind, leave the limited thoughts and beliefs and embrace your guidance. In doing so, be inspired to listen to that small still voice inside of you as it guides you to places you have never imagined exist.

Travel has always been a passion of mine. When I was married to my second husband, I'd asked him many times to take me away to someplace beautiful, and it never happened. So, I began to take trips with my friends and my sisters as a form of escape. I was becoming more empowered.

It was on one of these trips prior to my divorcing him that something very interesting happened and it was another sign that learning to listen to my inner guidance was going to be life changing for me. I messed it up before - and so God gave me a do over.

It was while driving to Colorado with my younger sister Allee and a dear friend, Judy that the conversation about soul mates started. My friend Judy had lost her beloved husband to cancer several years before this trip and they had been high school sweethearts. They were the ideal couple - the stereotypical small town football captain and the cheerleader. She was talking about her husband being her soul mate and how much she missed him and how she did not think she would ever marry again. We were driving through Kansas, and I will never forget the events that followed.

My sister piped in and said that she knew she was married to her soul mate. They had met when she was 17, and much to my parent's dismay at the time, they had rushed into marriage after knowing one another only a few months. Dennis had been in the Army and he and my sister married soon after he was released. Then, they moved to Illinois. My family was living in Colorado Springs at that time and our little road trip was my first trip back to Colorado - a place I adored, even after all these years.

The mood in the car was happy and we were looking forward to seeing the old house we had lived in when Allee and Dennis had met, and to visit some of the places we had loved so much when we lived there in the early 1970's.

So, why did I suddenly burst out in tears and say, "I know Ted is not my soul mate and if I ever had one, it was Jimmy, that boy from Harlingen."

I was driving and literally had to pull over off the highway. I could not see well enough to drive because I was crying so hard and big, gulping sobs were pouring out of me. The emotion seemed to come out of nowhere and was so sudden. My sister just looked at me with her wise eyes and said "I remember him and how much you loved him. Have you ever talked to him in all these years?"

"No." I managed to blubber out, "I don't even know if he is dead or alive. My life has been so wasted. I let him go because of this idea that I had of wanting security and now I have that and I am so miserable. My heart aches and it is too late to do anything. Maybe in my next lifetime I will do a better job and be happy." I then dried my tears, and we were on the road again with me apologizing for the sudden childish outburst.

Our conversation about soul mates had brought years of regret and buried emotions to the surface. I had certainly thought about Jimmy during the early years of my first marriage and my heart would race and I would dream of how it could have all been different. I often wondered if I should have married him, the one I adored, the dreamer, the artist. I felt deep down that we would have been OK, and just thinking of him would make me cry.

I thought at the time of my marriage that I had taken the easy path when actually, I had chosen unhappiness. Perhaps I should have followed my heart and married that boy I had loved for so many years—the one who lived 500 miles away. In hindsight, maybe I should have taken the bull by the horns and married Jimmy even though it would have been complicated. Instead, I chose the simpler road.

Now, I would never know and he would forever remain the one that got away – that sweet and sensitive young man I had left behind. He was still the one who made my heart race and my eyes tear up whenever I thought of him. In my heart, I believed that if only I could go back and do it all over again - I would make different choices and it would all be so perfect this time. If only.

So, back to the original question, "Did I make a mistake by not marrying Jimmy who lived so far away and who forever has a piece of my heart and soul?" I used to believe the answer to this question was *yes* and I thought that for most of my life. I thought of Jimmy often over the years with a smile and my eyes would still tear up. Jimmy usually crossed my mind when I was deeply regretting something and wishing I had made other choices. I thought of him when I was feeling sorry for myself and I often wondered if I had loved him as much as I thought I had or if he was as special as I remembered him to be. Was I just romanticizing the past? It had all been so long ago.

After high school, Jimmy didn't have a job that lived up to my expectations to support us in the manner in which I wanted to be supported. I was in my comfort zone, working at a cushy bank job. To further complicate matters, in order to be with Jimmy, I would have had to move to where he lived, about 500 miles away. I was afraid of living so far from friends and family. And, I was worried about not being able to land another job as good as the one I had. What if I wasn't smart enough?

And, Jimmy wasn't in sync with my timetable of getting a job and getting married. He was a soft spoken and slow moving young man who procrastinated in asking me to marry him. He was content with taking his time. He still is. I make quick decisions and don't have the patience he does. Sadly, I had grown very weary of waiting and so I began seeing someone else.

The man I decided to marry had a stable job that paid well at that time. I distinctly remember the day I wrote Jimmy a long letter telling him I was going to marry someone else and that I would always love him (yes, I actually wrote this in that letter). I was weeping, and I had to keep starting over again because the tears smeared the ink on the paper on which I was writing. Silly me, why couldn't I stop crying?

In the letter, I told Jimmy I would never be able to contact him again because it would not be right. I mailed that letter all the while hearing this little voice inside me crying out no, no, no! Jimmy and I did not part on bad terms. I never even gave him the chance to comment.

I will be completely honest with you here, writing that letter and not being honest with Jimmy about what I wanted in terms of status and material possessions became the biggest regret I ever had in my life. By allowing my fear to control me, I had let him go before I gave him the chance to talk to me about what I was hoping for and about what he wanted. We had two years invested in our relationship, and I hastily married a man I barely knew who I thought could give me the kind of life I wanted to have.

I was ready to get married - my first husband proposed, and it was convenient. He was a lot of fun and I loved him and I knew he was a good man. Strangely, I remember as we were heading to the JP to get married a few weeks later – we were both thinking about other people. I was thinking about Jimmy, and my soon-to-be husband was thinking about the girl he loved who was married to another man.

Life is ironic and sometimes, we must learn to pay attention to the things that keep coming up in our minds over and over again and pay attention to our God given gift of intuition.

By not being honest and direct and patient, I did not honor myself and my truth. I certainly did not follow my heart.

I am still learning the patient part.

When I married my first husband, my life was based on fear, and I allowed those fears to drive my actions. So, I married him instead of the person I loved with all of my heart. When I married my second husband, my life was still driven by fear and I was confused and lacked self - confidence and was looking for a new place to land.

Remember what I said about Divine timing? And the lessons we come here to learn? I know that if Jimmy and I had married, there would still have been lessons to learn. More than likely the same lessons would have presented themselves in different ways, or perhaps there would have been different lessons - but I had some things to learn about love and matters of the heart, all the same.

For you see we are given free will when we come to this Earth school, and we will make many choices during our lives here. We will make decisions that we think are right and also many that we know aren't the best ones. I have come to believe there are no wrong choices and that by marrying my first husband I took the path away from the young man I loved so much, and never stopped loving, because I allowed my fears to guide my actions. *Don't allow fear to rule your actions or you will remain stuck and never move forward.* You will be more apt to make poor choices if you allow fear to rule your life. Pretty simple.

Another lesson I learned from the time I spent married to incompatible people is that happiness dwells inside of us. It isn't created by our external worlds. Although many of us believe that the perfect marriage or the perfect home or having a great career or starting a family will make us happy - in reality other people and external things aren't the answer. In my experience - frame of mind, a sense of purpose, and loving ourselves and others will all help us to feel content.

A couple of months after my road trip to Colorado, I was in my closet cleaning and organizing, and a stack of old photo albums fell off a shelf and onto the floor. It turns out that there was a Divine plan working for me and Jimmy, even though we didn't know it at the time.

One album had a red and green plaid cover and I decided spontaneously to plop down on the closet floor to look inside it. I was thinking to myself, "I should have taken this to my sister when I picked her up in Oklahoma for our trip a few months before. I am sure it belongs to her."

Then, I opened the album only to discover that it contained pictures from the 70's, more specifically, pictures of Jimmy and me when we were about 19 and 20 years old. We took many of those pictures the day I left Harlingen to move to Colorado with my parents. I promptly burst into tears again.

Now this is where it gets a little strange . . . I heard a subtle voice in my head saying, "You need to find him." Yes, I swear that is exactly what I heard as I was sitting there on the floor weeping. Thank goodness I was alone in the house at the time. I thought to myself, what are the chances if I search for him on the Internet (social media wasn't invented yet) that anything will come up? So what were the chances?

As I was walking to the computer - I was telling myself how crazy I was. What was I expecting to find? What if he didn't remember me? Had I gone completely bonkers? Why was I doing this?

Even with all this chatter going round and round in my head, I found myself holding my breath and typing in his name and the city he lived in all those years ago.

Immediately - up popped a website showing Jimmy as the President of the Scottish Society. The listing showed an email address and even though I should have been terrified, I sat there for only a split second before typing in, "Hello, I am looking for an old friend from the 70's with the same name as yours who lived in Harlingen . . . "

You can only imagine my surprise after sending off that email when I received a reply back the very next morning. My hand shook as I clicked and opened the message. Once more those little voices chimed in "What the hell are you doing? You are opening up a can of worms. What if he thinks you are crazy? You ARE crazy. He won't even remember you." On and on the voices in my head repeated these thoughts, belittling me.

I opened the email and there he was – and he did remember me as I had been when I was 19 as the tall, shy girl with the long blonde hair and the heart shaped face. He recalled I had a sister named Allee and he wrote about his memory of me teaching him how to drive my brand new car that had a stick shift transmission so many years ago.

I smiled inside and out. I could not help it. I was reconnecting with a man whom I thought was lost to me forever. And it felt really, really good.

Jimmy's email suddenly brought back so many long forgotten memories. I thought of the times we had spent together walking on the beach at South Padre, his artistic abilities and the gift he had sent to me of a painting - discarded years ago by my jealous ex-husband. The painting had been of a beach scene we had enjoyed together. I recalled all the letters we had written to one another and the expensive long distance phone calls we made trying to hang on to our love and relationship for two years after I had moved from South Texas to Colorado.

More and more memories came flooding back. My heart ached for those times we had spent together. I longed to be happy again. If only . . . I had made wiser choices. If only I was not married. If only I could turn back the clock. If only I were young again. If only these things were possible.

How can I put on paper those feelings that surfaced that had long been buried deep down in my soul? I cannot explain it, but I will try. The moment I saw I had received a reply back from him I felt something I had never felt before. I felt my heart chakra open up, which felt like a flower was blossoming inside my heart.

I must have read that email 50 times. I was so happy, and I could not explain why. At that time, I did not understand energy and how we can have energetic connections to people and emotions and other souls. I did not know that the strange sensation in my heart was brought about by my pulling back to me a piece of my soul. I have since learned that our souls can fragment and we can leave little pieces with those we love. My soul was fragmented. It had become whole again after exchanging just one email.

Jimmy was my first, my last and my only soul mate and I knew we were soul mates the very moment we began to correspond by email. We had evolved over the many years into different people than we had been in our teens. Many of the similarities in our lives were astonishing. We liked the same things - travel, music, food, and movies. He was very much the romantic like me. We had purchased the same cars over the years. Our children were the same ages. The list goes on and on. If I didn't know better, I would think it was coincidence – but it was really Divine intervention.

We were both not happy with our lives and having trouble putting one foot in front of the other to make it through the day. We were uninspired and felt trapped in other people's selfish use of us. We were looking for the keys to unlock the prisons of our own making.

I still loved him and he loved me. What were we to do about it? I was struggling with tons of emotion and racing thoughts trying to figure out how to handle our situation. I was married, after all. So, I put my foot down that we would not talk in person and only communicate by email. That lasted a couple of weeks.

Unbeknownst to me (and this has to be based on Divine timing – right?) Jimmy had been searching for me and had been unable to find me. At about the same time all those tears were being shed in Kansas when I was thinking about my soul mate, Jimmy decided to try to get in touch with me. Uncanny, isn't it?

He told me about how he had been thinking about us and looking for me by my maiden name on his computer. This was before social media, and he could not find me nor remember my married last name, and then – all of a sudden – he received an email from me.

Memories of our time together resurfaced when Jimmy and his sister were sitting on his mother's couch going through a box of old family photos. His mother was ill and so he and his sister were at her house going through her personal belongings. He found a picture of me and pulled it out of the box. The photograph had been taken inside Jimmy's parents' house. I was standing in his bedroom, wearing a halter top and had my brown, leather-fringed hippie purse on my shoulder.

The picture made him laugh and he asked his sister, Linda if she remembered me. I think we had met only a few times, and she did not recall me. He told Linda that I was Pattie Lane, the girl that would not have to change her name if we had gotten married. Yep, no kidding - Jimmy's last name and mine were and are the same, Lane.

Here is the strange part, that picture cannot be found anywhere. It is almost like it manifested and disappeared into thin air. Jimmy has searched his things and the box at his sister's house numerous times. And, strangely, I don't remember ever having a photo of myself taken at his parents' house, but it may have happened.

I believe with all of my heart that Jimmy and I were brought together by the series of synchronistic events which occurred over about a three month period of time that included the drive to Colorado, finding the photo album and me sending off that fateful email. I believe our being together was a plan created by our souls before we ever incarnated in this lifetime. In order to fulfill our soul contract, a number of events happened as if by magic - and the pieces of the puzzle of our lives and our joint soul purposes started to fall into place as soon as Jimmy and I reconnected.

The process of freeing myself from my second marriage and the challenges of that situation took time and work and involved so many dynamics and setbacks. I had so many moments of doubt about whether Jimmy and I would ever be together in this lifetime. I questioned my sanity at times and so did many of my friends and family members.

The one thing I focused on that helped me hold things together during that time - was thinking about how I did not want to be facing the end of my life and have this huge regret that I did not put forth the effort to change my situation. I knew that even if Jimmy and I didn't end up together, that staying in my second marriage would be disastrous and I would never be satisfied being in the place that I was in at the time. I had to let the old life die and I had to create a place of peace and harmony. As long as I remained in the relationship I had with my second husband - that would never happen.

I began the process of divorce about six months after Jimmy and I reconnected. I moved out of the big fine home, took only my personal belongings and a bedroom set, and moved into an apartment close to where I worked.

Jimmy was working on us being together on his end also, and filed for a divorce about the same time I did. His divorce went through more quickly than mine did. After his divorce was final, he packed up his truck and came to join me in Fort Worth and that is where we currently live.

Thankfully, Jimmy and I did end up together and have been happily married since 2010. This book is not being written about our reconnection, though. It is being written to share the miracles that occurred to reunite us and what has happened as a result of our sharing our lives together.

The Angel's Orchestra

Chapter 9

Show Me A Sign

Sometimes we just know, and in knowing we have no choice but to follow our hearts.

One of the reasons I am certain that Jimmy and I are soul mates and that we are destined to be together in this lifetime is because we have received numerous signs and shared what could be interpreted as strange experiences. Spending time together helped relieve some of the stress and turmoil we were both experiencing during the trying time of detaching from our previous lives in order to move forward together.

I went through periods in which I was still torn about the decisions I was making. It seemed like everyone who was close to me questioned my sanity, and if the truth be told - I questioned it as much as they did. My brother, whom I had hoped to move in with temporarily, decided that he didn't want me to live with him. When I found out, I realized that my happiness and peace was my responsibility and I had to do this thing alone. My daughters were confused and hurt and worried about me. I didn't have the money to fight for what I was entitled to in the divorce settlement because I was paying rent and other living expenses and the constant stress depleted me to the point in which I had no energy to fight anymore. All I wanted was relief. Because of the emotional and physical exhaustion I was feeling, I decided to just give in and let my ex have it all. I simply could no longer fight as I put my fate into God's hands.

I felt guilty, hurt and betrayed once again by those I loved the most. I must confess that even though it sounds crazy, I was so consumed by guilt and fear and fatigue that I actually went back to the home I had shared with my husband and considered trying to make things work with him. The challenges of carrying the burden of being on my own without a support system, feeling hurt because my loved ones no longer respected me, and giving up everything I owned in order to move on were overwhelming.

Sadly, the stress and pressure were taking their toll on me physically, and eventually my body was unable to deal with it any more. The decision to divorce my husband was not one I made lightly. Eventually, my body reacted to the fear and intensity, and I suffered a stroke that paralyzed my left side. I was terrified that I would never be able to live a full life again, and I did not want to burden Jimmy with my health issues. I was also worried that I might not be able to hold down a job.

These were those darkest of days. At the time, I couldn't see clearly. The lesson I needed to learn was valuable and I had to fight to understand it. I questioned why Jimmy and I had been reunited if we were not supposed to be together.

I was torn about what to do and what I thought God wanted me to do. During this time, I was doing a lot of praying and asking for guidance from God and the Angels. My prayers were being answered, in Divine time – and the next steps in our miraculous journey were unfolding. I was gradually receiving true insight into what I needed to do.

It turned out that the only happiness I could find was when I was able to spend time with Jimmy. He made me laugh, and I found a place of peace with him unlike anything I had ever experienced. He was coming from a place of nonjudgement and understanding and absolute acceptance. The unconditional love he continued to offer me eventually helped me see myself and where I was going more clearly. I began to see myself through his loving eyes, to accept who I was and not be so harsh with myself. I felt like there was hope after all. He was my medicine and my light.

Because of his support, I found my way out of that darkness and I am forever grateful.

Shortly after Jimmy and I began seeing each other again, we decided to go to a Renaissance Festival a few towns away. Jimmy had come to town for the weekend, and we were just happy to be in each other's company if only for a few days. Jimmy loved to go to Renaissance Fairs, and I didn't know what to expect because I had never been to one.

Just inside the front gate, I noticed a brightly colored booth with a sign promoting psychics, palm readings and tarot card readings. I had never done any of those things,

The Angel's Orchestra

although there was a numerologist I had visited every few years for fun. I was amazed by how accurately she predicted events that would happen in my life during the several years I had worked with her.

I thought it might be fun to get a reading, and because I didn't have much extra money, Jimmy had given me some cash to enjoy some of the entertaining and unusual things the fair offered. I set my intention for this reading and hoped it would shed some light on what I could do to lessen my struggles and with that in mind - I decided to have my palm read.

I walked into the booth and went up to the first woman I saw standing by a small table. She just happened to be the palm reader and she was available to do a reading right then. Perfect! I promptly paid her and held out my left hand. She told me she wanted my right hand and instead of looking at my palm she asked me to turn my hand over so she could read the top of my hand. That was weird, I thought, but what did I know. I did what she asked.

Of course I wanted her to say something like, your soul mate has just come back into your life or you have a big decision to make and you must follow your heart. She didn't tell me what I expected.

Something even more spectacular than those words being said happened. In fact, it was apparent that a miracle took place that day.

As this palm reader and I were standing there and staring intently at the top of my right hand while she held it in her hands, a heart shaped image suddenly appeared on the fleshy area between my little finger and my ring finger. It just rose up. It was red and it was the perfect outline of a heart. It looked as though someone had drawn it with a bright, dark red felt tipped pen almost the color of blood only a slightly lighter color. This mysterious heart was there for about 20 seconds and then it suddenly disappeared. I gasped and so did she.

She looked at me and asked, "Did you *see* that?"

I managed to stammer, "Yes."

The palm reader was still looking at my hand as if she was expecting something else to happen, and stated in an almost breathless voice, "Well, that is very rare and I have never seen one before – I've only read about them. They are called stigmata." We were both in a state of shock. I thanked her and went back outside to Jimmy who was waiting for me.

I later learned that stigmata (singular *stigma*) is a term used by members of the Christian faith to describe bodily marks, sores, or sensations of pain in locations corresponding to the crucifixion wounds of Jesus Christ, such as the hands, wrists, and feet. Some Christian theologians believe that stigmata result from an exceptional poignancy of religious faith and a desire to associate oneself with the suffering Messiah. To be honest, I'm not sure that the shape on my hand was actually one. But, it doesn't really matter.

My goal for the reading that day was to receive some information that would help me to find my way through the suffering and confusion. I had been praying and asking for guidance. And there it was. My answer had appeared in living color and it took less than a minute. Love was winning in my life and I needed to stop overthinking everything and simply follow my heart. Faith is a wonderful thing.

The Angel's Orchestra

The whole thing was so strange and I cannot explain how it actually happened. I knew right then that it was definitely a sign. It was the answer I had been longing for. How could I doubt what I was doing when it gave me so much joy and something so magical had happened to answer my question? Seeing that heart on my hand gave me a little boost of energy and I knew right then that God and my Angels had my back. I would get through this and everything would be OK.

I was so grateful for this special miracle, but it turned out to be just one of many miracles that Jimmy and I would experience on our journey together.

Chapter 10

Healing the Healer

As healers, we must work from a solid foundation starting with a balance between body, mind and spirit.

I had received my message from God and it was time to take action. I made peace with my decision to leave my second marriage behind and to let love rule my life instead of fear.

In most situations in life, we have two choices. We can choose love and light and move forward or we can choose fear and rot in the darkness. I had done some pretty crazy things when I was in fear mode, but fortunately, things had become clear at last. I had chosen love and Jimmy and I moved in together to begin our new lives.

While I knew I had made the right decision, things were still tough. I was still having challenges with my health - struggling to find the energy to work at my job and recover from intense emotional wounds and physical pain. Jimmy basically took care of me while working a full time job himself, and he was doing most of the cleaning and cooking in our home. I was on a quest to find ways to get better so I could continue to work and have the energy to travel with Jimmy – and fulfill the dreams we shared. Jimmy kept telling me he would take me to see the world. I believed him.

Once again, I asked for Divine guidance to lead me in the direction I needed to move forward. One of the first things I felt like I needed to do to feel healthy again was to lose weight. I had become diabetic, and as I explored what my body needed, I was guided to follow a vegetarian nutritional program. This helped me lose weight and bring my blood sugars back into healthy alignment.

Becoming a vegetarian was life changing for me and Jimmy joined me, and that made everything so much easier. In the short span of 2 years - I lost over 100 pounds and was able to manage my diabetic condition with one medication instead of two. I had a little more energy as soon as I began to eat a diet that was healthier and provided what my body wanted, but I still wasn't in the shape I needed to be in to do the traveling Jimmy and I dreamed of doing.

I decided it was time to see a holistic doctor and explore more ways to help me gain energy and stamina. I also started to do research about regaining strength after a stroke and learned that many stroke victims have imbalanced cortisol and hormone levels. I also learned that when these systems are out of alignment, it can lead to the syndrome of Adrenal Fatigue, a condition rarely diagnosed or treated by traditional medicine. This really resonated with me and a light bulb went off.

The way I understand it, the adrenal glands pump cortisol into the blood stream to protect the body from stress overload. Cortisol is the flight or fight hormone that gave our ancestors the ability to survive during primitive times.

In modern society, cortisol works in the body when we are overwhelmed with stress. I had been afraid, fleeing and fighting for the past 25 years, so my adrenal glands had been working on overdrive. When we are under duress for long periods of time – as I had been, the adrenal glands become overwhelmed and can simply burn out.

Taking multiple medications can also affect the production of cortisol. I had been taking massive amounts of prescription drugs since the stroke and this factor also contributed to my adrenal fatigue.

One of the medications I was taking in large doses was the anti-depressant Adderall. It had been prescribed by a psychiatrist to help me have more energy and treat my chronic depression. Adderall functions like speed and I discovered through my research that one of the side effects is adrenal damage. When I learned this, I stopped taking the medication and after thinking it through, realized it hadn't really helped me. I then learned that when the adrenal glands are tired, we also have a shortage of the sleep inducer melatonin. No wonder I was exhausted all the time!] It made perfect sense to me that prescription drugs are chemicals and chemicals create imbalance in the body and taking multiple prescriptions throws off the chemistry of the body and this stresses the adrenal glands. Ding, ding, ding!

My journey to wellness continued when I found an amazing holistic osteopathic doctor named Dr. Karen Birdy who ran a series of tests, confirmed I was suffering from adrenal fatigue, and promptly put me on bio identical hormones, thyroid medication, and a supplement to rest my adrenal glands. I was grateful to have found Dr. Birdy, a doctor who finally listened to me when I described my symptoms. Her professionalism and immense knowledge about the human hormonal system put me on the road to recovery.

Dr. Birdy also recommended a book to me titled "Adrenal Fatigue—The 21st Century Stress Syndrome" by James L. Wilson. I am sure there are many more books on the subject – however, I continue to recommend this one to my clients. It is a good sized book and contains several checklists and references to doctors who treat Adrenal Fatigue. I still drink the salt water and the licorice tea it recommends. I learned so much from reading this book.

Adrenal fatigue and its accompanying conditions are life disabling. I cannot explain what living with this type of weariness is like. Let's just say I was not living. I was sleeping my life away. Quick cures and magic pills do not exist. The road back to a normal life is a complicated journey.

Fortunately, I had taken the first steps to get well and I finally had hope that someday my body would recover and I could live my life my way.

During this time, I continued to be mindful of nutrition. I was well on my way to becoming vegan and I began to eat organic foods as much as I could afford and started juicing. I eliminated all sodas, most caffeine, and stopped drinking tap water. I began to drink lots of herbal tea and added as many fresh herbs to my diet as possible, especially basil as it is good for the adrenals. I completely eliminated bread, pasta and baked goods. I even started a meditation practice and started listening to my body. I also became more balanced and did not overwork myself as much.

Baby step by baby step, I began to feel a little better and continued to tweak my diet by adding a few supplements like vitamin B, C and D and iodine for my thyroid. I noticed I would have more good days during the week. Not every day, but a few days a week was motivating and I slowly began to feel like doing a bit more. Shortly after my stroke, I would literally sleep for days trying to get my energy back. When my energy began to stabilize, I didn't need to sleep nearly as much and this was a huge thing for me because I felt like I was going to be able to lead a normal life once again. I stayed on the synthetic Cortisol for about 2 years and really took care of my body and eliminated as much stress from my life as I could. I went from full time to a 35 hour work week, making the necessary adjustments in my lifestyle so I could take care of myself a little better while surviving on a little less income.

My goal was to become well enough to get off all the prescribed medicines I was taking. I especially wanted to stop taking prescription blood thinners. Something had to change, and I had begun to realize that I had to be the one to take my health into my own hands.

If you research and think you may have adrenal fatigue, find yourself a doctor or holistic practitioner you resonate with who understands this ailment and can treat you as you will more than likely be seeing them for a long time. Take the time and the money and the effort it takes to get well as it is well worth the effort.

A half lived life is a half full life. You deserve a full life and it takes energy to live that kind of life. I still suffer with intermittent energy limitations, but I do have three times the energy I had when I was very ill. I am extremely grateful for my recovery. I now lead a full life, despite those limitations.

Through trial and error, I have discovered that energy management is the foundation on which me living a full life depends. I am now aware of how much energy I spend each and every moment of every single day and of the things I experience in my life – people, situations, surroundings, nutrition, etc. that deplete or replenish my energy. This has made me do a better job of managing what I allow in my life and what I avoid. I view my energy much like a bank account. And so, I make deposits and withdrawals in a mindful way. If my life force energy account becomes depleted, then I simply stop spending and take the necessary steps to replenish it.

Deep down, I had faith that I had experienced these challenges for a reason. My healing journey taught me many lessons, but most of all – it eventually inspired me to work as a healer so that I could support others on their physical, mental, emotional and spiritual journeys. I used my new found energy to train and study and experience even more miracles.

The Angel's Orchestra

Chapter 11

Archangel Magic

Michael, the Fierce protector
Gabriel, God's messenger
and my special friend, Raphael, the healer.

In my metaphysical ministry, women come to me for spiritual counseling, intuitive readings, and energy healing. It is interesting that we spiritual healers often attract clients who are facing the same types of issues or who have comparable needs to ours. Many times, people come to me who are plagued with similar or even the very same illnesses I have encountered in my life. If you only learn one thing from this book, understand this - we are better healers if we can empathize with our clients and what better way to empathize than to have encountered the same situations the client is going through in our own lives?

Remember when I said that there is always a reason we experience what we do? Even if at the time we simply cannot comprehend it. I believe we are all healers to one another and healing happens in many ways, shapes and forms. We are all healers to one another. Hold that thought for a moment. That is just the way of things when you are on this path and you truly care about others. This journey of healing ourselves and helping others all works together magically and mysteriously.

Facilitating the healing journeys of others is an honor and a privilege and I am constantly learning and training to improve my craft. Since I have progressed as a healer, I am now often led to read a certain book or attend a specific seminar. I've also discovered that while I am fortunate to be exposed to incredible instructors, learning with other students and hearing about their experiences and lessons is a huge benefit.

About six months after my health had significantly improved, so I decided to take my first Reiki energy class. I was hoping it would help me to feel better and I was becoming fascinated with energy work and reading a book by Eric Pearl titled "Reconnective Energy Healing."

I am a healer and I went through a rigorous process to be healed physically, mentally, emotionally and energetically. I needed to understand it all and learn how everything works together. And, I had to comprehend it thoroughly enough so I could assist others, or at least give them some guidance in exploring and finding ways to heal themselves.

During my healing and learning endeavors, I was blessed to encounter Archangel Raphael. I was well on my way to feeling better when the miracle of Archangel Raphael entered my life. I share this story which is another one of those magical and mystical experiences I do not fully understand. This experience changed my life and this is how it happened.

In July of 2012, while driving in downtown Fort Worth, I had the most amazing experience while stopped at a red light. I had the radio booming, was gulping coffee, and was focused on getting to work. I glanced into the lane next to me and my eyes were drawn to the top of a city bus and the bright letters showing the name of the street that was its next destination. It said RAPHAEL as plain as could be in *big bold green capital letters*.

I looked away, and having lived in Fort Worth most of my life, my immediate reaction was, where is Raphael street? There's not a main street in Fort Worth with the name Raphael that I know of. Looking back, the letters had changed to say Rosedale. But, I had seen RAPHAEL only a second ago. My heart skipped a beat.

OK, I now understood enough about the metaphysical workings of the Universe to realize that this was a sign from above and not to be ignored. While I have been given some profound guidance from the Divine in the past, I have not ever looked with my physical eyes at something in writing and *seen* something else.

At the time, I didn't even know what Raphael meant. I knew I needed to find out because this was clearly an important message for me to heed. It was Divine communication at its best, and it had my full attention.

I also felt my energy buzzing and was caught up in the excitement around this sighting. It was all very surreal, and I sent up a prayer for more signs and messages . . . please.

Reaching my office within a few minutes, I immediately called my husband and told him what had just occurred. I recall feeling high and happy for some reason, as if I was on the edge of discovering something amazing. The hairs prickled on my arms as I asked, "Jim, do you know what Raphael is, what it means?"

"I think it's one of the Archangels." he replied. "Why don't you Google it."

I must stop for a moment and mention that I had recently been certified as a Reiki 1 practitioner and had been reading a book on energy healing for about the fifth time. I was considering traveling to California to become certified in this additional energy healing modality and had been trying to find ways to come up with the money. Energy work and helping others resonates with me to my very core. As a metaphysical practitioner, I am always looking for additional tools to add to my healing tool belt.

So, with this in mind, I wondered if Raphael might be related in some way to healing and energy work. When I did the research, I learned that Archangels are assistants to God and exist in every major world religion. They each have specific expertise and perform certain functions to help humans. When I received my answer to the question about Raphael - it blew my mind to discover that Raphael's specialty is healing! Actually, Raphael is a HEALING MASTER! Whew! I quickly sent up another prayer for more guidance before I jumped into my work day.

I was not expecting that guidance as soon as it came. When I walked into my house after work and turned on the TV, I could not believe it! Right there in front of me was a documentary about three Archangels. I had not even had time to flip through the channels!

The Archangels being discussed in this documentary were Michael, Raphael and Gabriel. The information was based on old religious texts and the documentary was beautifully composed with many paintings, statues, and spiritual locations and references in spiritual texts around what was being referred to as "The Band of Mercy Angels." There were also many stories of people who had seen these angels and experienced miracles in their lives.

Wow, this was the second really clear and profound sign I had received in one day! I got it. God had my full attention.

I began to cry and felt strange. It was as if I was having an out of body experience. I asked, "why me?" and I heard in my right ear very clearly an immediate answer to my question, "You love Angels, look around you. You love Angels and we are going to communicate to you through the Angels."

So, I dried my tears and looked around my living room as I was asked to do. There, I found bookcases full of books about Angels, and my eyes were drawn to the curio cabinet holding most of my Angel statue collectibles and then to the wall above our TV where Soul Solace hangs.

Soul Solace is the picture Jimmy painted for me soon after we first reconnected. It is a scene in a Celtic village depicting our souls wrapped around each other ascending to heaven while a band of Angels below us holds lanterns in their uplifted hands. He knew how much I love angels - always have and always will. This message was further validation that I needed to pay more attention to the Angels around me. Jimmy's painting, Soul Solace is on the cover of this book!

I had my second sign and I asked for another because, I knew that three signs pretty much seals the deal!

A few days later, I received an email from a friend of mine who I consider to be a mentor. She is a spiritual teacher and a life coach, and I have known her for several years. She was my Reiki 1 teacher. Her name is PJ Spur, and her work is life changing. She also wrote an amazing book that helps people navigate through grief. It is included in a list of books I highly recommend at the end of this book. You should also check out her husband, Steve Spur's book. He is a medium and one of my teachers as well. I am forever grateful to have Steve and PJ Spur as teachers, and even more importantly as personal friends.

The email PJ sent to me was an invitation to join her at a workshop in a few months taught by Charles Virtue. It was an extensive workshop built around his mother's Angel Therapy certification class to obtain knowledge and experience around connecting with Angels and to learn how to receive/channel messages of validation for others and be certified as an Angel Practitioner® - the name of Charles' certification program.

I now had my answer, even though it was different than I had originally expected – but that is how most Divine things come about! Many times, you think you know what you want and you think you know how you should receive it. I'm here to tell you that you can't out guess God's plan, so be sure not to put limitations on Divine guidance. We will talk more about how to receive Divine messages later.

I decided to go to the workshop with PJ and not surprisingly, this workshop changed my life. Prior to attending, I did not know who Charles Virtue was and had never read any of his mother's books. I did not know there were angel cards and certainly did not know how someone would go about *reading* them. I did not believe I was an intuitive person. This was all so different and kind of way out there for me, but during this part of my journey, I was learning to have faith and trust the guidance I was receiving. I was also learning to walk through the fears - one step at a time.

And so, I followed my intuition and the signs I had received and I took that leap of faith and signed up for the class. I had no idea what to expect. I ended up in this class simply because I recognized that I had been guided to it. I did not have the money on hand to pay for the hotel, food and the workshop. I needed over $1,000 and that was a fortune for me to come up with at that time.

I knew I had to just trust and go for it, because the guidance was so clear. Sometimes we have to surrender and follow the signs because that is when the real miracles happen. After all, I had learned the lesson about how to receive and recognize guidance when I was working with the palm reader - and it brought the miracle of peace and a *knowing* that everything would be OK when reuniting with Jimmy. Fortunately, I was beginning to learn to trust the process of Divine intervention even more!

I finally made the decision to put the workshop on a credit card and I am so thankful that I did. On the four hour drive to Houston, PJ and I stopped to get drinks and snacks and the entry road back onto the freeway was a few miles long. Along the roadside, buzzards were everywhere. We literally saw dozens of them. PJ looked over at me, smiled and said in her wise voice, "This is going to be a transformational weekend. Buzzards mean change and transformation." Who knew? Not me, but I was learning.

We checked into the hotel, went to dinner and came back to head to bed. I was excited and did not sleep well. I dreamed that night that I was flying (without an airplane).

The next morning Charles and his assistant rode the elevator down with PJ and me. I did not know this, because I had never seen him before and did not know who he was.

P J and I walked into the breakfast area and discovered a room full of mostly women, of all ages and ethnicities who shared one thing in common. We all loved Angels. This was going to be fun!

The morning of the first day of the workshop was mostly lecture. There were more than 150 angel believers in that room. The energy was really high, and I had never been in energy like that where I could literally feel it in my body before.

PJ and I bonded with several women during the breaks, and a group of about 15 or 20 of us made plans to go to lunch together. Many of the women were already reading cards professionally and Charles had invited a few of his personal friends who were professional readers to sit at the back of the classroom and provide readings for those of us who wanted them. I did not get a reading as I did not feel I could spend any more money.

I really enjoyed the women we had lunch with, though, and two of them were doing the readings for the class. Several women had come to the workshop from other countries. One woman, had taken Reiki in England and been attuned at Stonehenge by William Rand himself. These women all seemed to have been blessed with the abundance to travel and really enjoy life. They appeared to be fearless and very devoted to their studies and their angels. I loved them all, and I have become personal friends with many of the women I met in this workshop.

Charles talked a great deal about the importance of developing and using our intuition to help others. He spoke about doing this work for others and about how we should charge for our services. I could not imagine at that time that I would ever be intuitive enough to charge for readings. At the end of the first day I felt like I was way out of my league in this room full of women who traveled the world and even read cards professionally.

On the second day we returned to the classroom and found a deck of cards for each one of us on our table. There were several different decks lying on the tables, and the one I received was in a large blue box. I looked at the deck and was intimidated but curious. It was The Angel Tarot deck and was the first deck that Doreen Virtue created based on the traditional Tarot. I bonded with the deck so much during class that I use it as my primary deck whenever I do readings for clients. I also base my card reading workshops on this deck.

Charles gave us some pointers about how to do card readings, and we practiced doing readings with other students after that. I was surprised that I was able to pull information and give guidance more easily than I ever imagined. "I think I can do this," I thought.

On the third and final day of the workshop, more mystical and magical things started to happen that were difficult for me to wrap my brain around. Actually, after experiencing those events, my life would never be the same. It started when Charles told us that we would be channeling Angelic messages and not using the cards we had been given.

"What!" I thought. "Not use the cards. Now, how does this work?"

We were told that we all have the ability to do this work if we just trust and say what we see, feel, hear and think. We are like telephones. We also learned that we had to surrender to whatever messages we received, and not focus on being accurate. Charles told us that we needed to be responsible and that part of doing this work properly is to deliver whatever we get – we just say it, but in a kind and gentle way.

As we continue to practice, and gain experience, we will develop a working relationship with our Angels and be able to receive more information. He asked us to sit in front of the person we were *receiving* for and imagine our Angels above us communicating with their Angels. The way we connected with the person we were reading for was by asking our Angels to join with their Angels and them saying their name out loud three times. I did three of these channeled readings that day.

During the first reading, I held the hands of a lady as she said her name three times. I immediately saw a horse in my mind's eye - as clear as could be. The lady confirmed that she owned many horses and worked with children who had special needs. It was a type of therapy for them. I was amazed.

The second reading was also interesting. I was reading for a man and when I closed my eyes I saw a rough log fence running along the edge of a mountain range. It was spring and the green grass was tall. There was a beautiful blue sky with floating clouds. That is all I saw and I gave that information to the man and he just smiled and said, "Well, OK". I must admit I felt like a failure, but then I remembered that Charles had said that we couldn't have attachment to whether or not the messages were correct, so I just let it go.

It was almost time for lunch, and Charles had been standing at the front of the class while we were doing our readings. He was out of earshot and didn't hear my second reading. He said it was time to break, however he wanted to share one more thing with us before we left for lunch and this is what he said.

"Once when I was learning to channel without cards I had a person in front of me and when I closed my eyes all I saw was a split log fence in a meadow of tall green grasses with mountains in the distance on a sunny day. There were puffs of white clouds in the sky. That is all I saw. I did not understand. So I asked for more and the picture zoomed out in my mind to show more. I saw a little girl sitting on the ground with her back to one of the posts in the fence and she was crying. There was a book on the ground next to her. I knew that this was the place that the woman I was channeling for would go to find solace from her unhappiness. She validated that."

"What I want you to always remember is that you can ask for more if you do not understand the image or the words or feelings that you are receiving. You can ask for it to be shown to you in another way. Just remember to ask if you do not understand what you are receiving."

I looked around the room for the man who I had just read for. He was staring at me and shaking his head in amazement. I know - it was pretty bizarre. Charles had not heard our conversation as he had been nowhere near us when I was working with this man.

It is the third reading I did that day - the last one - that is the most memorable, and my motivation for writing this section of the book. To this day, this reading stands out as one of my all time favorite miracles and every time I share the story – both I and the person with whom I am sharing it feel the Angel bumps appearing on our bodies. The Angel bumps appear every single time.

Angel bumps are energetic signals and reactions to the importance of words. They feel similar to the shivers that run up our spines or the raised hairs on the backs of our necks when we encounter danger. When I receive and share information during a session that is especially important or significant, I often feel those energy bumps along my left arm or up and down my spine – and so does the person to whom I'm speaking. I call this response – angel bumps. These physical reactions validate the importance of whatever message is being received and conveyed.

The woman I was reading for is named Sherry and she has given me permission to share this story. I am going to present this story from Sherry's voice first and then mine.

Sherry's voice

"I truly believe in synchronicities and feel there are no accidents in life. I feel blessed that you are part of my life. As I recall, we were discussing how Archangel Raphael came into our lives and what signs he presented us to show that he was helping us.

In my case, my daughter Kaylee, was having a big grand mal seizure and was turning blue due to respiratory distress. I had just read the book, "Archangel Raphael" by Doreen Virtue, so was fairly new to angels at the time. I asked Archangel Raphael to help Kaylee and to give me a sign that everything will be okay.

The paramedics came and Kaylee was stable again. We were rushed to Driscoll Children's Hospital just for safe measures. I'm an RN so I was thinking of all the things I needed to do like get Kaylee admitted, plus oxygen machine for home, oxygen for home, rescue med, and etc.

The Angel's Orchestra

We were waiting in triage when a lady walked into the room. She said, "Hi, I'm Raphael." I said, "Excuse me, what is your name?" And she said, "I'm Dr. Raphael." In that moment, I felt the goose bumps, tears rolled down my face and I knew that everything was okay. I felt this peace wash over me and I surrendered all my control and just let things be.

Dr Raphael gave us a rescue drug just in case and told us to follow up with a neurologist on Monday. We were sent home and I was okay with that decision. Kaylee slept the rest of the afternoon and all night. We lived on a canal and I noticed that three pelicans swam near our dock for two nights just circling around our home.

I knew Kaylee was in good hands, and that I didn't need to worry. It was a great feeling that Archangel Raphael was the real deal and that Kaylee was going to be okay.

Ever since that moment, I have been a true believer in Angels - and eight months later I met you at the Charles Virtue workshop."

My voice

A lady sat in front of me and I closed my eyes and asked my Angels to talk to her Angels as she said her name. Almost immediately, I envisioned a young girl with long blonde Shirley Temple curls, running up and down a set of stairs that were in the middle of a room all by themselves. She was laughing and saying, "Look Mommy I can walk. Look Mommy I can run."

The woman in front of me said, "This is not for me, let me go get the lady, Sherry, who sat next to me today for you. I believe this is for her."

She brought Sherry to sit in front of me. Sherry was a beautiful young woman with dark hair and a slight Asian appearance. I questioned my vision/message for her but remembered Charles adamantly telling the class over and over that in order to do this work and become a stellar reader, then we must gain the courage and confidence to say what we are getting and not make judgments of any kind.

Sherry said, "I think you may have a message for me."

I took a deep breath, closed my eyes and saw the very same scene and repeated to her what I had seen both times.

"I see a blonde girl with long curly hair running up and down a set of stairs looking over her shoulder laughing and saying, "Look, Mommy I can walk. Look, Mommy I can run. She looks very happy."

I opened my eyes and Sherry had tears in her eyes. "Yes, that message is for me. That is my daughter Kaylee and she cannot walk unassisted. She was born with a genetic disorder, 1P36 Deletion, which affects her muscles and leaves her without the ability to walk without assistance. The fairness comes from my husband, and, Kaylee has long blonde curly hair."

Wow, I thought. I am so grateful that I just said it. What an amazing vision. Thank you, Angels.

It gets better.

Sherry's voice

"There are many miracles and blessings. I had just come back from a Hay House I Can Do It Conference in Washington DC in Sept or Oct of 2012, so Doreen Virtue and Brian Weiss were both fresh on my mind when this happened at the Charles Virtue workshop.

When I got home from the conference I came across Charles Virtue's workshop on Facebook and I did more research on it. Originally, I wanted to attend a Doreen Virtue workshop, but I believe she wasn't offering one at the time. I attended Brian Weiss's workshop on Friday at the 'I Can Do It conference' and sat next to a man. I forgot his name. We did a psychometry exercise where I gave this man my watch and he held it in his hands. He told me an image came to him where there was an older lady with a black shawl and asked if that rang a bell. It didn't at the time, but I thought maybe he was referring to my grandmother but I didn't remember the black shawl about her.

He then mentioned a little girl climbing up the stairs with a blue dress and a clock or maybe a bell. I wish I had written this all down so I could remember all of the detail."

My voice

It was October and I am always cold. I reached behind me on my chair and pulled the black shawl to show it to Sherry.

Another unbelievable synchronistic event had occurred. Sherry had been guided to meet me and receive a reading.

"How are these things even possible?" I asked myself. I could not and still cannot completely wrap my mind around the synchronicities of this event or even the steps that were clearly laid out to lead Sherry and me to this time and this place. Even after all these years and all of the training and all of the mysteries of the world that I've seen and experienced – this one still stands out.

I cannot begin to understand how much orchestration it took for our Angels to get us together, for all of the steps leading up to Sherry being in the place she was led to be, and for inspiring me to attend this workshop.

The lady sitting next to Sherry sat down in front of me when there were about 150 other people in the room that she could have sat down in front of. I have lots of jackets, but I took the black shawl. Sherry's Dr. was named Raphael. Raphael had guided me to this workshop. The miracles go on and on.

Sometimes it is best to allow ourselves to just believe and give our Angel's permission do their work. Faith is a marvelous thing. So is staying out of the way and surrendering to the magic of the Divine.

If you are in need of healing or believe yourself to be a healer, ask Archangel Raphael to come into your life. Ask him to light up your path. Ask him to show you how to begin the journey of healing yourself. Ask for miracles in your life, magical synchronicities and clear signs. Ask all in the name of God and make a promise to help others and be of service when you are able to.

To be honest, I sometimes question this process, but deep down I know that trusting it is often the best thing. I know one thing for sure – the fact that Sherry and I met each other was not an accident.

For Sherry, this incident propelled her to move forward on her journey to explore even more holistic and alternative ways to help heal her daughter, Kaylee. She continues to do so today, and Kaylee is improving by leaps and bounds.

Sherry has become an activist and a powerful voice in the fight to find a cure for this rare disease which, many times, takes the lives of the children who are afflicted with it. The message of the image I saw in my mind's eye gave Sherry hope and motivation and courage to do what she now does.

After the workshop, I knew I would be working with the Angels, doing readings, and helping others. Just think, if I had not jumped in and gone to this class, and if the Angelic guidance had not led me to this place, and if PJ had not invited me to go with her - I would not have had those experiences, and may have never known that I could do this work. The series of events that happened and led me to the workshop inspired me to serve others as a metaphysical practitioner and teacher.

This is the perfect example of a Divine calling. The experience gave me the final bit of validation that I was being steered and encouraged to do this type of work.

Chapter 12

Answering the Call

If we can dream it we can bring it into our lives.

The Divine had clearly intervened in my life and called me to work as a healer using my intuitive abilities. Even though I was interested in spirituality and had been studying metaphysical subjects for many years, I mostly did it out of curiosity and to help heal myself, and not to fulfill a certain purpose.

Another interesting thing about the workshop is that the night before that last day of readings that changed my life forever, I dreamed I was flying. At the time, I didn't realize that when I dreamed of flying, it had a certain meaning. And after I returned home and was able to meditate on what had happened, I remembered a similar dream I had several years before that workshop.

Although I did not know it at the time, it was a prophetic dream which foretold what was to come into my life in a most miraculous way. Like many of life's mysteries, I had the dream at a certain point in my life, but I didn't fully understand its meaning until years later.

The dream was so very powerful for me and although I did not journal my dreams back then, I did take the time the next morning to write this one down in detail because it was so vivid and the sense of urgency to deliver the messages in the dream was strong, even though I did not know what I was delivering. I felt like this was a dream I needed to remember.

Before I arrived home on the very night in which I had the dream, a really scary thing happen and I called upon my Angels to help me. I was on my way home from a party at a friend's home in an unfamiliar town. I was driving in the dark, and came upon fog so dense that I could barely see the light from my own headlights in front of my car which was completely encased in the thick blinding fog.

Soon after leaving my friend's home, I discovered that I was lost, had no idea where I was, and was worried that I would be unable to find my way home. This was during the time when cell phones had just been invented and most people didn't have them yet, so there was no way for me to call for help. And because I was unable to see any of the buildings on the road, I couldn't stop and find a pay phone. It was dark and cold and creepy. I was terrified. I asked my Angels to surround my car with protection and show me the way home. And miraculously, I arrived home safely shortly thereafter.

That same night I dreamed I was flying over the mountains with Angels by my side protecting me. Below me, I could see campfires scattered throughout the mountains. Somehow, I knew that my mission was to land and deliver special information and messages of encouragement to the people who were sitting by each fire. I felt safe, but also had a sense of urgency that I should deliver the messages and move quickly on to the next campfire.

As I flew over the treetops, I could look down and see so many little glimmering lights from each camp. I knew that when the messages were all delivered, I would land on top of a mountain, on a large flat rock that formed a platform. At the end of the dream, I finished my mission and felt satisfied by what I had accomplished.

Several years later, I began studying dream interpretation and learned that this particular dream held two messages for me. One message was showing me that I possessed information that would help others. Perhaps I needed to be of service in my community, because I had the necessary tools. The dream was also be telling me that one of my missions in life was to assist others.

The second message was, of course, to remind me of my ability to fly and that whenever I took a leap of faith, I would be safe and be able to soar. I did take that leap of faith and I do so every single day. I now deliver messages of healing and inspiration with the guidance and support of my Angels.

It is important to emphasize how powerful dreams can be. Dreams are the Divine's way of communicating with us while we sleep. The predictive dreams I had as a child were an early indication about my heightened intuition. Because they didn't understand the spiritual world, my parents believed that they were protecting me by teaching me to be fearful of my dreams. As a result, I became reluctant to acknowledge my gifts, became less sensitive as time progressed, and unfortunately repressed them for most of my life.

Encourage your children to talk about their dreams and share their dream adventures with you and to never be afraid of dreaming. Every night before going to sleep, I ask my Angels to be with me and protect and guide me and you can teach your kids to do this also. Many times intuitive gifts are discovered through the dreams we have from an early age. And, don't ever be afraid of the messages that dreams contain, they are gateways to the Heavens and can show us so many things. There are no earthly limitations when we sleep and no time, space or boundaries.

The future can be seen in dreams, past lives can be visited and we can travel anyplace in the world, past, present or future. We can meet our guides and our Angels and visit with our departed loved ones when we are sleeping and dreaming.

In dreamland it is possible to find the answers to all those questions that are bouncing around in our heads during waking hours. We can heal our mental, physical and emotional bodies during dream time. Don't ever discount dreams and the messages that lie within them. Peel away those layers of the onion and be open to the metaphorical messages they contain. And, be aware that your Divinely inspired dreams can awaken you to your own special life purpose and provide information about how you can be of service in this lifetime.

After I returned home it took me some time to process everything that had happened during the workshop. I eventually heeded the messages to use my intuition to help others, but not before I had a long talk with God and my Angels. I told God I would do this work on certain conditions.

I asked for the messages to come easily and be valid. I asked to be given the courage to do this work, and to be put in the places I needed to be in order to deliver messages. I asked to be able to read for others with my intuition because I did not have the time or the energy or the inclination to study traditional Tarot for years. I asked for my gifts to be strengthened and requested that I be a conduit, and that I be used in whatever capacity God wanted to use me. Lastly, I asked to be well again so I would have the energy to follow this guidance and be of service in the highest capacity possible.

In the silence of meditation, I received my inspiration and a few months after I completed the Certified Angel Practitioner workshop,

I was delivering professional readings at one of the largest fairs in the nation alongside some of the most highly regarded readers in Texas.

My Angels certainly knew what they were doing when they led me down this path, and I am happier and more fulfilled than I ever thought possible. And that is what life is really about - finding balance and that happy place. I still practice Reiki and teach others and my perceptive and healing abilities grow stronger each day as I experiment and just go with my intuition.

My real passion now is communication with God thru his Angels and sharing that experience with others. After all, the Angels are his messengers. I am a channel for Angelic messages and for this I am eternally grateful.

Another important lesson that I've learned through years of experience is that I shouldn't ignore a sign or a message because it is not revealed or delivered to me in the manner I expect. Whenever I'm not sure if what I experienced is a sign, I simply connect with my Angels and ask for more guidance or ask for clarification in another way. I've also learned to be patient if the answer doesn't become crystal clear immediately. Experience has taught me that I will be led and the knowledge will be given to me when I am ready and it is time to take the next step.

In addition to opening ourselves up to Divine guidance and timing, we must also trust that God and the Angels know what they are doing. I've learned to just observe and follow the signs I am given. Trust is the key here, and you can learn to do it too.

The Angel's Orchestra

Chapter 13

Working with the Masters

According to the high lamas, no one ever attained Enlightenment without the help of Goddess Tara.

Things really took off after that first metaphysical fair. It went so well that I began to seek out other venues. It didn't take long to find them, and within about four months, I was working at other fairs doing readings almost every weekend. I did this for about two years while still working at a full time, corporate job. My energy levels were getting better every day.

One of the regular practices I developed in order to do my healing work and maintain the energy I needed to juggle so many things at one time was to meditate every day. Meditation has so many benefits, and they are too numerous to mention here, but for me meditation has become not only a gateway to harmony and balance, but also provides access to new Divine messages.

I invented the Sacred Spaces Pillowcase, after being given the vision and instructions to make them during a meditation. It was 2013, and I was so very busy with work, reading cards and sewing my precious

The Angel's Orchestra

prayer pillowcases with hidden pockets in which to store scraps of paper with prayers for ourselves and others, dreams and inspirational messages written on them as well as energy healing crystals.

I felt motivated to slow down a bit, to find more time for myself and spend more time at home and to travel with Jimmy, but I loved earning extra income for travel and spiritual classes. I was still on fire and earning a respectable name for myself as one of a handful of Angel card readers in the DFW area who read at local fairs. But, also, I was yearning for more balance in my life.

It was while in meditation one morning that a strange thing happened. Very clearly in my mind's eye, a dazzling dark green being appeared and floated up in front of me. She had a jewel in the center of her forehead and the most beautiful features. She was smiling. As she was levitating in front of me, her legs were extended below her torso and resembled a fat snake with green, red, and gold stripes running around them. They appeared to be encased in baggy pants and it was the colorful stripe on the pants I noticed that reminded me of the snake. Her words to me were so simple. "It is time for you to begin to teach."

Whoa! What? My mind immediately reacted, "I don't know enough to teach. I am only beginning. I am not ready to teach."

She smiled and said, "You know enough to begin and you can continue to learn. There are many people who are beginners just starting on this journey, and they are looking for a teacher who can relate to them and teach at a simple level. It is time for you to begin to teach and you will begin with Reiki."

Reiki? I was not even a Master and I had very little experience in practicing Reiki. I had purchased a Reiki table and had a few regular clients, but I did not offer Reiki healing services when I was at the fairs—I read cards instead. This was really confusing.

Was I supposed to add yet another thing to my already overflowing plate? I must admit that I thought about this for only a short period of time. So, I sent up a prayer and asked if this was real and valid guidance. I requested that my Angels step forward and prove it to me. I asked who this Green Goddess was. I asked for signs and validation, as I had learned to do over time – just observing until the answers became clear.

A few days before seeing this green being during my meditation, I had ordered a new deck of cards to add to my ever growing collection. The name of the deck was The Goddess Guidance Oracle cards. That deck of cards was delivered by mail three days after I had received the message from the green Goddess in my vision. I had never seen this deck of cards before, and had no idea what was in them, but they looked really nice. I enjoyed collecting new cards and they had been on sale. So, there they were.

I remember this just like it was yesterday. I opened the deck and as I do whenever I work with a new deck, I turn over the cards one at a time. I also touch them and study them and feel their energy. And, all of the sudden - there SHE was. I stopped breathing, and I probably made a sound of some kind.

Jimmy was sitting in his recliner and he looked up questioningly. I had already told him about the meditation and the message I had been given the morning it had occurred.

I remember saying, "You are not going to believe this. That Green Goddess that came to me the other day is in this deck of cards. She looks exactly like she did in that vision. She has striped pants and her skin is dark green with a jewel in her forehead. Her name is Green Tara. I have never heard of her before, but here she is. Can you believe that?"

Once again, I didn't know how this had happened or why, but because this wasn't my first rodeo as they say - I began to think it might be time, once more, to hold onto my hat because if history was any indication, even more miracles were sure to be on their way.

So, true to my nature, I started doing some research on the Green Tara that day. I was eager to discover who she was and why she had come to me. It turns out that she is very sacred and very real.

I learned that a Tara is a female Buddha, a manifestation of the ultimate wisdom of all of the Buddhas. Tara has 21 major forms, each of which emits a different color and represents a special spiritual attribute and energy. Of these 21 forms, two are especially sacred to the Tibetan people. White Tara who is associated with compassion and long life and Green Tara, associated with enlightened activity, healing and abundance.

The name Tara means star. One of her many messages is to empower us to save ourselves. The Green Tara is also the healing aspect of Tara, and each of the 21 Taras is an expression of the principal Tara, Green Tara.

We can turn to Tara, for refuge. She protects us from all internal and external dangers, she provides us with all the necessary conditions for our spiritual training, and she guides us and inspires us with her blessings as we progress along the spiritual path. We can call upon her, and she will come to us in the most interesting ways.

Green Tara is the Mother of all Buddas. She is Tibetan and also known as "Dolma or Mother of Mercy and Compassion. She is commonly thought to be a protector who comes to our aid to relieve us of physical, emotional and spiritual suffering. The green Tara is the Bodhisattva and not only embodying compassion, is known by the practitioners of the Tibetan branch of Vajrayana Buddhism (the Diamond Way) to assist in developing certain qualities and in understanding the inner, outer and secret teachings about emptiness.

I was floored and could not get this incident (synchronicity) off my mind. I asked for more signs as I was still a little hesitant about the teaching guidance I had received from her. I knew that I was experiencing a significant spiritual event, and my eyes were open wide.

Prior to her coming to me I did not know who Green Tara was, just as I did not know who Archangel Raphael was when he made himself known to me. In the next 6 months I was to encounter Green Tara so many times that it became almost comical. Immediately and for the next several months, I met so many Tara's and came across so many Tara related articles in magazines I picked up and places I visited. I will share with you here a few of those more comical encounters with you.

Besides having a dozen or more Tara's and Terra's come to me as clients and sit in front of me for readings, Tara interacted with me in other amusing ways so she would be noticed. After living in the area for several years and never noticing it before, Jimmy and I discovered a neighborhood close to us named Tara Estates. It is a small community of plantation-like homes and even boasts its own pharmacy, The Tara Pharmacy.

Shortly after this happened, we were on a trip to Colorado where I picked up some nice handcrafted soaps in a small boutique on one of our outings and looked at the label and nearly laughed out loud. They were called Tara Soaps. A few months later, we were in a store in Sedona, AZ looking through a bookcase of used books. My eyes were drawn to a small green pocket book way up on the very top of the bookcase lying close to the edge and I felt compelled to reach up to get it. It was the Green Tara Handbook. Over and over things continued to happen to remind me that the Green Tara was close to me energetically. I had received the validation I had asked for in a big way and realized that I would indeed, begin to teach.

The Angel's Orchestra

And so I began teaching little workshops about reading cards and how to develop intuition to students who were just embarking on their spiritual learning quests. I also put into place the steps I would need to complete in order to be qualified to teach Reiki through the International Center for Reiki Training which is William Rand's organization, as I was so clearly being led to do.

Of all the spiritual things I have been so clearly guided to do, sharing what I have learned by teaching may be the most fulfilling and the easiest thing I have ever done. Green Tara was right. Teaching has helped me to evolve further on my journey as a healer and the extra money I earn from this work I adore has enabled me to travel more than I ever dreamed of doing.

In 2015 I went to Sedona for an International Reiki Retreat which was held in what I believe is one of the most beautiful places on earth–The Mago Resort. While there I had been looking for a bronze Green Tara statue, but could not find just the right one. Trusting my instincts, I came home without one knowing I would find the one that was meant for me at the right time I was meant to find her.

The previous year, Jimmy and I decided to take a trip to Ireland. It was a dream come true for me. I had always wanted to go to Ireland. So many Divine miracles happened on that trip. I met a little old man in the pub and he mentioned my daughters' names and explained to me that I would write a book and that I just needed to do it. And, another memorable experience occurred on the drive up to the Hills of Tara when I literally felt my heart chakra opening up again.

Within a few months of my trip to Sedona, Jimmy and I answered our longing to visit Ireland once more. I found myself at my beloved Hills of Tara again and was honored to meet the famous Celtic artist Courtney Davis who owns Hill of Tara Open Studio, a tiny stone cottage housing his art studio, metaphysical store, and upper floor classroom at the base of Tara.

It was the afternoon before the Super Moon Eclipse, and Jimmy and I had planned this trip around the momentous lunar event. I was grateful and excited to be at my hill to bring in the energy of this special moon.

I happened onto Courtney's studio by chance and Divine synchronicity. I do not believe it had been open the year before when we were visiting Ireland. I walked through the door, and there he was - this artist whose work I had just been admiring in the café gift shop a few doors down.

As I entered, he looked up to greet me and I recognized him from the tiny picture on the back of cards I had been considering purchasing in the nearby gift shop. I did not know what to say. I looked around and his artwork was everywhere.

I don't know what we initially said or how we ended up by his tiny fireplace sitting across from one another. There was no one else in the studio and Jimmy had gone out to the hill to meditate and pray as I grabbed a quick bite to eat and walk around the dirt road exploring the shops located below the hills.

Courtney and I began to talk about spiritual things and I told him how I had physically felt my heart chakra open up the first time when driving up to this sacred place and how much I loved it and felt a deep spiritual past-life connection.

I told him how fortunate he was to have a studio at the Hills. In my mind's eye, I even saw myself walking these hills in long robes lifetimes ago. I told him about my connection to Green Tara and shared the Green Tara meditation experience. I told him how much I loved her. I asked if he knew if she was somehow connected to this place with the same name.

He confided in me the first painting he painted was of Green Tara and pointed behind me and there she was. He told me that two major ley lines crossed one another where we were sitting. I realized that like the energies of Sedona, I felt the energy of this ancient sacred site just as my ancestors had.

Ley lines are apparent alignments of land forms, places of ancient religious significance or culture, and often include man-made structures. They are ancient, straight 'paths' or routes in the landscape and are believed to have spiritual importance. This is evident in Ireland where the Hills of Tara are located, and a church was built on this site in ancient times over ancient worship sites. The energy of ley lines is significant, and for whatever reason, ancient peoples were able to sense the sacred energy and were attracted to build places of worship there. Christians then followed the example and built on ley lines over the pagan sites.

As he Archangel Michael ley line and the Mother Mary ley line ran right below where we were sitting I could feel their energies. I have not done research on this other than to read about the Saint Michael ley line running through Ireland. Ley lines fascinate me and I literally know when I am near one. Courtney and I talked for about an hour and no one disturbed us.

We talked about many things and when it was time for me to go I wanted to purchase some things in his store to remember this amazing day by. I began to browse and my eyes were drawn to a tall glass shelf where a bronze statue about 8 inches tall sat. I had found my Green Tara at The Hills of Tara. How very perfect was that? I was grateful I had listened to my guidance in Sedona and waited to find the perfect statue at the perfect time and in the perfect place. It pays to be patient. Sometimes things work out better than we can ever imagine.

All I had to do was travel all the way to Ireland to meet the man who painted the pictures of Green Tara and other Ascended Masters. I picked her up and Courtney mentioned to me that she had been in his personal collection for many years and she was very old and for some reason, he had felt like it was time for him to sell her. He had reverently placed her in the case just a few days earlier. We both knew that she had been anticipating my visit in the magical place named after her.

I now had my Green Tara statue and several pieces of Courtney's artwork. Of course, the Green Tara print was among my treasures and both the statue and print are with me now and I cherish them every day when I see them in my home office.

The miracles of the Green Tara are very sacred and I do not share them lightly with you. In fact, Courtney cautioned me to be careful with whom I shared this with because what I experienced was very sacred and should be treated with reverence. I know that everyone who reads this story has a special need to connect with Green Tara and believe that magic is everywhere inside of us and surrounds us in our everyday lives. I also know that this book will find its way into the hands of those who are meant to read it and who are ready to benefit from all the experiences I share here.

I am certain that Angels, Goddesses, Spirit Guides and Ascended Masters all work together and even though this book is titled "The Angel's Orchestra" and is based on the description of what my Dad heard when he crossed over; I know there are an endless number of helpers on the other side working together for our highest good.

Connect with them. Ask for their guidance. Do it now.

The Angel's Orchestra

Chapter 14

Mediumship

Communicating with the departed is another Divine miracle and with the assistance of the Angels, it heals in miraculous ways.

So many mysteries occur in our lives, and Mediumship – the ability to see and communicate with those who have died, and share their messages with their surviving loved ones - is one of these magical things for me. As happens frequently with many mediums, I discovered that I could see and communicate with the departed suddenly and unexpectedly.

It started happening about a year after I started doing intuitive readings. I would just be in the middle of doing a reading, and suddenly someone would step in. I actually see the physical appearance of the departed person in my mind's eye. And, for some reason, I know that they are coming through from the other side of the veil. This has

The Angel's Orchestra

happened on rare occasions, and I usually have no warning and no control on when it occurs. After they appear in my mind's eye, the visitors begin to show me things. What is really interesting is that often right before that spirit comes in, I draw a certain card in my deck which seems to trigger or be related to these events.

The first time it happened, I was reading for a young woman at The Dallas Psychic Fair and I laid this particular card down. BOOM! A man then suddenly appeared to me. He was heavy set and Cajun. He was sitting, and his appearance was very much like the image in the card I had selected. He was laughing with his head thrown back, and I could hear his big old belly laugh.

I looked at the young woman and said I thought there was someone on the other side trying to make contact and it felt like it was her Dad. I told her this man was Cajun. I heard the words 'baby girl' as clear as could be. I told her he called her baby girl and said she was a dancer as I could clearly see her dancing and twirling. She looked at me in shock.

It was her Dad. Everything fit. She was visiting the DFW area from her home in New Orleans. She was involved in theater and danced. The last thing he said to tell her was that he knew she kept his picture on her night stand and she did.

After that incident, I decided to take a Mediumship class with my friend Steve Spur aka The Cowboy Psychic. He is real good at what he does and occasionally teaches workshops in the Dallas-Fort Worth area. It was important for me to have a good teacher who spoke in simple terms. Steve is a good 'ol boy and has some amazing gifts. I like him because he is easy going and laid back. I refer people to him often because he speaks in layman's terms and puts people at ease and had no ego around his gifts. Steve is authentic, honest and ethical. His book is listed on my page of recommended books at the end of this book.

Steve's Mediumship course was one evening a week for about three months. After a few weeks in class, I was awakened in the middle of the night to a spirit knocking on the wall above my bed. I heard three knocks and then silence for a few seconds and then three more knocks. It happened over and over and was so loud it woke me from a deep sleep.

What the hell! I thought and I don't curse often. I just knew it was a spirit waking me us. Now, I was scared. I just was not going to develop my Mediumship abilities if doing so meant that my private space would be invaded. I value my sleep too much to be awakened from a deep sleep by some crazy spirit. I don't enjoy being scared either.

I said, "Go Away." I am not going to be awakened from a deep sleep like this, and I will not do this work if you scare me. Go away now." I pretty much made it clear that this was the end of that. The knocking immediately stopped.

I called Steve the next morning and told him what had happened. He asked me how I reacted to being awakened by the event, not sounding surprised. I don't think too much surprises Steve. He laughed when I told him what had happened and asked me to research the Fox sisters who spoke to spirit by means of knocks on the wall. He said they were responsible for the Spiritualist Churches of today. I did the research and afterwards, I must admit I felt that I may have over reacted and acted in haste when I scolded that spirit. After all, hadn't it been communicating in a way that would have been understood by most mediums who have studied this subject?

But, I did not invite spirit back in. Steve told me I could do that if I changed my mind, and they might or might not come around again. Steve also said that I should always remember that I am the one in control.

I had no incidents or visits from spirit for about 6 months. Then, one day, while reading at a different fair, I laid that same card down and realized I hadn't pulled it for a while. I looked at the woman in front of me, for whom I was doing the reading, and immediately saw a tall young man standing next to her with a cowboy hat in his hands. He held the hat out to me in a beckoning way and then he did the strangest thing. He drew and X on that cream colored hat with a huge black marker. Next, he showed me his cowboy boots which he seemed to very proud of and then placed a red baseball cap on his head.

It turns out that this young man was this woman's departed son. I had never had so much validation, even more than the dancing girl from New Orleans and her father. This woman's son loved his boots, but would not wear a cowboy hat and his job required him to wear a red baseball cap.

I could sense his personality and described it to his mother, and also described to her how he had passed over in an accident, how he dressed and how reckless he was. He told me to tell his mom that he was making a lot of bad choices during that time right before his death, and she confirmed this. She validated everything. In the end he spoke about one of his sons, calling him his "mini me."

At the end of that session, the woman hugged me and thanked me for what had taken place. I remember we both had tears in our eyes.

I had not even invited spirit back in. But, how do you say no after an experience like that? I had to pray and think hard about this line I had drawn in the sand with spirit.

I told my Angels and guides that I would do this work for them only on my terms and if they ever allow knocking on my walls again or if they allowed anyone or anything to scare me, then I would ask them to leave again. I was real firm and then I just let it go. I asked them to be my gatekeepers. You get the picture.

After this incident, people and animals began to come more often when I was reading. They gently stepped in and still do with the utmost respect. Now, the visits are not scary and they come only when I invite them into my space. Oh, how I love working with spirit in this unique way.

Recently, I was doing a phone reading and the spirit kept showing me her beautiful hands and the ring she wore. When I mentioned this to the young woman for whom I was reading, and whom I had never met in person, she gasped. The spirit was her mom and the young woman was wearing her mother's ring that day. Although I could not get a clear picture of the ring on her hand, I could see the woman clearly and she was beautiful. I could also sense her energy which was loving, gentle and protective toward her daughter. I can't explain it. I just say what I see, what I feel, and what I hear when spirit steps in.

The Angel's Orchestra

The more Mediumship experiences I have had, it seems that the amount of information increases and the detail I am able to see improves. Recently, while doing a reading, I was shown a man coming into a room that was a library with what looked like books on the shelves. He said they were not books, but a collection of some sort. These large volumes of books appeared to be sorted on the shelves in a very specific way. They were in fact, a collection – it turns out that this man was a stamp collector.

Another interesting thing about this particular reading is that before he came into the room -there were a bunch of dachshunds wagging their tails and jumping up and down excitedly. The first one was a tan color and a female. It turned out that the man was a dachshund breeder. The light colored one had been a favorite of his. Whimsical surprises like this make me enjoy this work even more, and I really like it when the animals pop in on a regular basis.

When I connect with those on the other side, people who have been with me in person say that the features and the appearance of my face changes, and it begins to morph and turn different colors. I don't know about this, and afterwards, I don't typically remember too much that comes in. But, the good news is that it doesn't scare me anymore. And, it offers me a special kind of opportunity to help others.

Another sign that I should further develop my Mediumship abilities came to me not through a client, but from a dear friend. Lane Robinson is a psychic medium and energy healer whom I met after she and I had both commented on something that our teacher, Charles

Virtue had posted on Facebook. For some reason, Lane and I felt a connection and started communicating on social media. It turned out that Lane had also taken Charles' Certified Angel Practitioner® class – but at a different time than PJ and I did. She also had a life changing experience during the class – she discovered her own Mediumship abilities.

Even though Lane and I communicated through social media for quite some time, we didn't meet in person until almost a year later when Jimmy and I were taking a trip to Colorado. Lane invited us to her house for lunch and prepared a gorgeous French onion soup – vegetarian style. We hit it off immediately. Several months later, out of the blue, I received a phone call from Lane.

She was sobbing so hard I could barely understand her and after I asked what was wrong and urged her to take some deep breaths, she said, "Pattie, I need your help. I just found out that my 26 year old nephew, Eric might be dead." It turned out that Lane's family was estranged and that her other sister's son, Eric's cousin – had seen a post on Facebook a few days earlier with messages that said "RIP, Eric." Eric's cousin told his mom about the post and Lane's sister called to see if Lane had heard anything. No one had contacted Lane, either.

Eric's mother, the third sister, had not spoken to the rest of the family for many years. Lane didn't know what happened with Eric, and she needed clarity. She and her sister had a feeling that Eric had taken his own life because there weren't any posts on Facebook from his parents or other family members, and they couldn't find an obituary online. Lane was understandably very distraught and that is why she called me.

The Angel's Orchestra

I was working my corporate job and didn't even go through any process to connect with spirit. I just picked up the phone when it rang. Immediately after Lane told me what was happening, in my mind's eye, I saw a large white letter "D." It turned out that Eric was a HUGE fan of the Denver Broncos football team, and the big white "D" was their logo. The Broncos had won the Super Bowl that year, so it was not a surprise that Eric showed me that logo. I also saw the color orange, lots of orange.

I told Lane that I was getting the name "Daniel." She told me that Daniel was Eric's middle name. I was able to confirm that Eric had taken his own life and he wanted us to know that he was highly evolved spiritually when he told me "This isn't my first rodeo." He also let me know that he was ok now and there was nothing Lane or anyone else could have done to prevent his suicide. It was a short conversation, but Lane knew right away that I had spoken with Eric and that he had transitioned successfully to the other side.

Recently, Jimmy and I visited Lane for Thanksgiving at her home in Santa Fe, New Mexico where she moved to expand her metaphysical practice. She shared with me how much that reading nearly a year and a half earlier had meant to her and she gifted me a special reading to repay the fact that I read for her with no notice and without charging her. It was funny because when Lane reached out to me for help, she just needed some comfort, and I was the first person who came to mind, but she didn't know I was a medium as it is not something I have accepted or actively promoted.

During our visit, she told me that she believed I should pursue Mediumship because of the ease with which I received messages, the accuracy of those messages, and especially because of the way I approach the work as a healer and deliver messages gently and with grace.

I had not been representing myself as a medium before because I was unable to turn this gift off and on and hadn't had the level of training I thought I needed. I've reconsidered, though and decided to study Mediumship further so I can learn how to control how and when I receive messages and to improve my reading skills so I can add Mediumship to my healer toolkit.

Until I feel ready to promote these services, I figure that my Angels and spirit guides have my best interest at heart and will continue to be my gatekeepers by bringing in the spirits who need help, and asking those who do not meet my specifications to go away.

I will say that working as a medium is very rewarding and I have formed some special bonds with those clients whose loved ones choose to appear to me. Recently, I was at a fair doing readings, and I looked up and recognized the mother of the cowboy with the cowboy hat in his hand and the red baseball cap on his head. She was bringing her son's "mini me" to meet me. I was honored to meet her darling grandson. It was the highlight of my day. I see her often when I work at fairs in that town. It is interesting, though that her departed son has not shown up for us again. Spirit works in mysterious ways.

Mediumship is a special type of metaphysical magic. When someone describes the process of talking to souls on the other side, it can sound weird and scary. But actually, when I work with my Angels, it isn't strange at all, and tremendous healing often happens during those readings.

One of the things that the Mediumship experiences have taught me is that my work as a healer will always be growing and evolving. And, I am learning to be open to Divine timing and intervention as I continue to pursue this path as well as the signs that lead me to a certain healing modality or practice.

Chapter 15

Past Lives and Dying without Regret

Live a life of purpose and you will have nothing but gratitude at the end of your days.

I don't know about you, but when I leave this earth, I want to leave with as few regrets as possible. I want to be able to look at my life and know I did my best and did not allow others to negatively influence my life path nor to pull me away from my purpose. I want to know that I led a life full of love and joy and not a life dictated by fear and regret.

In order to do this, I step through fears on a daily basis. I ask for miracles on a daily basis. I ask for guidance on a daily basis and I ask how I can be of service to others every day.

In order to develop a healthy perspective about death and dying and living a full life, I recommend a really great book called "The Top Five Regrets of the Dying" by Bronnie Ware.

Bronnie was a palliative care professional and worked with people at the end of their lives. She lived with them in their homes during their transitions, and therefore became very close to her patients and their families. Bonnie possessed the gift of being a great listener. As she spent more and more time with people just before they crossed over, she began to recognize a pattern - that her patients were sharing similar stories around their regrets about their lives.

Listening to the repetitive themes of her patients' regrets, she soon became aware of how she was living her own life, and what she might regret if she didn't start to pay attention. She then set a plan into motion that included the steps to do those things she desired to do in her own life.

The time we spend on this Earth is so short and goes by so very fast. Read the book. Even more important, make your bucket list and begin doing the things you want to do. This is one of those things you do not want to procrastinate on too long. Do this today so that you will not take a long list of regrets with you at the end of your days.

The most important first step is to let go of your fears. In order to fulfill some of your desires, you may need to release limiting thoughts, beliefs and fears.

As you know, after my dad's NDE, I was propelled into studying spiritual things. As a result of my studies which quickly became my passions, I came to believe in reincarnation. I can't explain why. It just resonated with me at a deep soul level.

I began to read everything I could about reincarnation including all of the books by Brian Weiss. These books blew me away and led me to read others.

Shortly after Jimmy and I got back together and right after I took my first Reiki class, I decided I wanted to experience a past life regression. I was looking for validation that Jimmy and I had lived past lives together.

Who better to actually regress me than my Reiki teacher, P J Spur? P J had been doing PLR's for several years so she had lots of experience and I trusted her which is very important when choosing someone to take us on this intimate kind of a journey in which we can feel exposed and vulnerable.

I booked a Past Life Regression session with PJ, and here is how that went.

I recall being little nervous because I did not know what to expect, but PJ quickly calmed any concerned thoughts I had. So, I trusted the process and thankfully, I was able to experience two past lives in this two hour session that day.

In the first lifetime, I saw myself as a man living in the Holy Land close to the time of Jesus' life. I was a shepherd, lived a very simple life and knew what was important. My family and the love I had during that lifetime far outweighed any of the luxuries I did not possess. I was content and at peace. On my deathbed, as I gazed into the eyes of those who loved me - I recognized my sister in that lifetime as being one of my sisters in this lifetime.

Lisa and I have a special bond, are both spiritual seekers and have experienced many things together in this lifetime. She is my very best friend. She is the one I admire most for her strength and her ability to forgive. I love and admire her life and what she has overcome would fill a book. I admire her strength so much that I am planning to write a book about her story and the power of forgiveness. My sister Lisa, is my hero.

In the second lifetime, I was given a glimpse of Jimmy who was my beloved brother in that lifetime. We lived someplace in France, near the ocean in a huge white home that had been left to us by our parents in the late 1700's. I was married and had children. My husband in that lifetime was my second husband in this lifetime. We lived a comfortable life and owned ships that imported and exported goods.

My brother, Jimmy, loved the sea and although he would have been fine helping to oversee our estate his love of the ocean and sailing kept him away much of the time. When he was home he lived in the large family home with my husband and I and our children.

I recall hating for Jimmy to leave us and sail away on those ships. I recall how much he meant to me. I believe we may have been twins with that close connection only twins have together, although I looked up to him like a big brother. I must admit I loved him more than anything in the world.

One day he sailed away. I stood on the deck watching my handsome brother walk up the plank and onto his ship carrying a large white sack over his left shoulder. This vision was as clear as could be and I also recall the emotions I felt around his leaving once more.

Jimmy's ship did not return when it was scheduled to return. I recall going to the docks day after day looking to the sea and willing him to return to me. I realized he was gone and I did not get to say goodbye. Jimmy and his ship had gone down. He had drowned at sea all alone.

I passed from that life years later of what I believe was a broken heart while standing on that dock outside our shipping building longing for him.

I began to cry before P J brought me out of that regression session as the feelings of love and loss overwhelmed me. I knew those emotions well as I had felt them deeply in this life time too. And then, the feelings of sadness and abandonment I had felt only a moment before simply disappeared as PJ brought be back to the present time. We discussed the lessons of those two lifetimes and how I could use what I had learned to live my life to the fullest in this lifetime. It was a powerful session.

I was still processing all I had experienced from the PLR session as I pulled into the driveway. Jimmy was home and I could not wait to discuss my Past Life Regression experience with him.

When we were able to sit down and talk about what had taken place during the regression, something amazing was brought to light. As I told the story of our owning a shipping business, Jimmy's passion for sailing and described the ship he sailed off in with its' numerous sails and complicated looking ropes he looked intently at me and confided his lifetime fear of the ocean and inability to swim. He told me he had an intense fear of drowning and just knew he had drowned in a past life. He told me about how he had owned a small 2 man sailboat and shared with me his love of sailing despite his fear of the water and drowning. He had sailed often in the bay between the South Padre barrier island and Port Isabel in his tiny sailing craft because the depth of the water was relatively shallow. I also recalled that the first date we had was in Corpus Christi on a schooner sailing around the bay area and how Jimmy had looked as he took over the ship's wheel at the invitation of the captain.

Then, Jimmy got up and walked to the closet in our home where he stored the painting supplies and pulled a picture of the ship in my vision out of his painting closet. This picture had been painted as a young man more than 30 years before we reconnected. It was one of his first paintings, and it was painted on a huge canvas with lots of detail. Wow, I had not known of this painting's existence.

By now you know that I always ask for validation and for proof when I encounter spiritual messages and experiences. I had not even asked for validation of this past life to verify that what I had experienced in the past life regression was real. How would you prove that those things which happened hundreds of years ago actually did happen? And yet, here was confirmation of this past life when Jimmy was my brother all those years ago in the physical form of a picture he had painted as young man.

When I do Past Life Regressions for my clients, I often ask them to return to the time they passed over in the lifetime they are visiting and to tell me what they see as their greatest accomplishments why and what brought them the most joy, then I ask them to tell me what they regret not doing in that life time-what they would do differently and then I listen.

One of the last things I ask my client is if they were able to share a message with the world, what would that message be and what were the most significant lessons that they learned during that lifetime? I am always humbled by their answers.

It is always easier to see where you are going when you know where you have been. I know where I have been and who I was in more than a dozen past lives through past life regressions with different PLR therapists. Some of them are famous. Yes, I did get to experience a past life regression with Brian Weiss, more than once and my certification is with one of his protégées, Shelley Kaehr.

I am honored Shelley is my mentor, and that she shared her knowledge and experience with me. Meeting her was an unexpected opportunity which I acted on quickly when it presented itself. Becoming friends with her was a bonus and is such an honor. I am so grateful for the role she has played in my development, and for her placing her trust in me.

I am always touched and I am always honored to be doing past life regression work. Many times, I am compelled to ask my clients to project themselves out into the future to the end of this lifetime and to tell me if there are some things they feel they will be regretting which have not been accomplished, completed or resolved.

They never say they regret not having had enough money or the finest clothes or home or car or even a successful career. At that point in our lives these things will not be important. What I hear are statements related to forgiveness, and being more patient, loving and kind. They voice regrets about holding on to bitterness, grief and guilt; about not loving themselves and not forgiving themselves and others more; and about living their lives to please others, and not for themselves. They regret they did not have the courage to move through their fears.

They regret being too afraid to lead an authentic life because of what others may have thought about them and allowing their limiting beliefs to keep them in prisons of their own making. They say they regretted spending the precious time in this lifetime working in an unfulfilling job. They state they should have moved through all the fears that held them back from doing the things they really wanted to do in life. Fear is a major hurdle we must jump through if we are to live the life of our dreams.

This is a partial list, but you get the idea. Many things we believe are so important, we realize at the end of our lives are not that important, after all.

Living a life with no regrets is dependent on loving ourselves and stepping through our fears. The more we are able overcome fear, and love ourselves, and put into practice those things our heart desires, the more we enable ourselves to live a full life and to fulfill our dreams and leave this life with fewer regrets.

Chapter 16

Life's Lessons

Nothing is random and all things we experience in life have been set into motion for Divine purpose...

So many things I have learned on my journey thus far have been valuable to me and I feel obligated to share them for the greater good. Each one of these lessons by itself is life changing, but when they are combined – major miracles happen.

I've included them in no particular order. I invite you to reflect on the ones that resonate with you the most and practice them in your daily life.

Lesson One – Take Care of Yourself

This is probably the most important lesson of all, and it was the most difficult for me personally. I recently was proud to tell my angels that I had learned self love. This does not mean I cannot learn to love myself on a deeper level. I wanted them to know I was working on this one really hard and I was aware of how important it is.

My angels came back with the message that since I understood this I was to share that message with others and empower them to recognize the importance of loving ourselves enough to build a solid foundation on which we can fulfill our purpose and contribute to others. They told me that self love is one of the keys to manifesting.

Loving ourselves includes taking care of our health – mental, physical, emotional and spiritual; satisfying our own fundamental needs first so we can support others from a firm foundation; and acknowledging that we are valuable and that we are worthy.

When I was unhappy and fearful, I felt so pressured to take care of everyone else's needs and to even deny my own. I didn't even think about the concept of taking care of myself first. The Divine intervened and I had a stroke and Adrenal Fatigue which put me on an educational journey in which I learned to love and take care of myself. I learned to treat myself how I would treat a close friend – if I wouldn't feed them something, talk to them in a certain way, neglect them or beat them up with negativity – I learned not to ever do those things to myself either.

Self-love means believing that we are worthy of receiving – both Divine gifts and the support of others. In order to make a significant difference in the world, we also must love ourselves enough to recognize that we are valuable and the fact that we are on the planet contributes to the greater good.

Today, some of the things I routinely do to practice loving myself are eating food that nourishes my body; practicing meditation; praying and trusting the Divine and my Angels; using positive self-talk; accepting compliments gracefully; believing that I am worthy because the loving light energy of the Divine lives in my soul. What a difference these changes have made in my life. I now receive so many blessings.

Lesson Two – Live a Full Life

Living a full life basically means choosing love and light and happiness and joy instead of darkness and fear and guilt and making choices in our lives that support this. It means letting go of the past, living in the moment and being optimistic about the future. It also means understanding your strengths and knowing that you are a powerful soul made up of Divine light and energy - visiting this Earth in a human body. It also means taking care of your energy and living at the highest possible vibration for yourself and the planet. You embody God's sacred spark next to your heart. That spark must be fanned into a flame in order for you to live at your highest potential.

Ways to live at a higher vibration include eating whole, organic food; avoiding negative media such as television and radio news; staying hydrated; not complaining, practicing positive self-talk; and living with a sense of excitement.

Now, this is really important and I hope you get it. One of the most important first steps toward living a full life is to become aware of your thoughts and your feelings. It is important to understand who and what you really are and what makes you unique and special. For you are a powerful soul experiencing a human lifetime in order to more align your soul with your Divine purpose. You are here to expand your awareness in order to help other's realize who and what they are. Align your thoughts and your feelings to your high calling and your highest desires in order to maintain your vibration level.

Another big issue that can lower our vibration and keep us living unfulfilled lives is guilt. This was another hard one for me. I often laugh and tell people I came into this world with a bunch of guilt. I even feel guilty for things I have never done and for other people's actions. I have learned to let most of that go. I advise you to let it go too. It will eat away at you and you will make bad decisions like I did when I gave my ex-husband everything in that second divorce. It is much easier to let go of guilt once you work on loving yourself and it is much easier to love yourself when you leave the baggage of guilt behind.

Living a full life means doing what is important and not procrastinating and putting things off to the point that they never happen. We must learn the difference between patience and procrastination and the way these two feel in our bodies, because they are different. Patience is giving things time and procrastination is putting off something we know in our hearts will have to be dealt with. There is a difference and only you will know that difference by how the energies of these two different things feel in your body.

We must learn patience and as I mentioned before, patience was a hard one for me. In patience I have learned that I truly receive what is in my highest good. It is that simple.

Finally, living a full life means living in peace. Living in the now is where we find peace. Living in the now with intention and purpose is where we find joy and happiness. Living in the now while living a purposeful life and opening our eyes to the magic that our Angels can provide us with is where we can find bliss.

Lesson Three – Pursue Your Purpose

As we have said throughout this book, our lives on Earth are meant to be lived with purpose and to be enjoyed. I believe that many times we limit our thinking and our beliefs and our expectations and we start living our lives in a box and we never find the key to open that box. I know so many people who get out of bed each morning and drive to a job they hate and come home to an unhappy household and think that life is drudgery, and they just need to put one foot in front of the other and survive day to day. They do not live in joy and they do not think about living to be of service to the planet and to pursue their highest purpose.

I want you to go to work to discover your life purpose and understand what lights you up and what you are passionate about. I want you to ask God and his messengers to help you with this and then keep your eyes open for the metaphysical signs. This book has given you many examples about how I learned to pray and ask my Angels for signs and then how those signs appeared. You can begin today.

We must learn to put forth the effort to live a life that is all our own and authentic. The first step is to learn to love ourselves enough to make this happen and to know that we all, each and every one of us, are here for a higher purpose than just to survive and work our lives trying to accumulate wealth and prestige. Those things will not belong to us when we leave this earth and will disappear. We must realize that no one else can or will do this work for us. It is up to us to begin this journey and the journey will be different for each one of us.

Finally, if you are having a difficult time figuring out what your purpose is and where to start the process of finding it – there are teachers and tools at your disposal. You can use more quantitative metaphysical tools such as numerology and astrology in addition to working with Angels.

One thing I learned was that one single decision can profoundly impact our live purpose. I decided to take that class with PJ and Charles Virtue, and BAM – my life purpose began to reveal itself and in such amazing ways! When the student is ready, the teacher will come and the more open you are and the more you desire to discover and achieve your purpose, the sooner it will happen for you.

Lesson Four – Have Faith

Another big lesson I've learned on my journey is that it isn't all up to me to make everything work. A powerful Divine force is present in my life and in the lives of those people who simply believe in the possibility. One of the reasons I lived in so much fear is because I didn't acknowledge all of the Divine assistance that was right there next to me – if only I would ask. I had my team of Angels and they have always been there and will always be there to help. I must admit that it is easier to have faith when you see evidence of it working, but you can't make that happen until you take one initial leap and just trust that things will work out.

Fear is probably the biggest enemy of Divine energy. Divine energy is love and light and fear energy is dark and debilitating. The best thing you can do to take advantage of Divine blessings is to just stop being afraid and ask the Angels to help resolve whatever things in your life are making you afraid. When we live in fear, we are dwelling on the failures of our past or projecting our thoughts and feelings into worrying about the future. Do you want to focus on the future, a place you cannot really see with all the energies of the unknown?

Remember when I was trying to decide to marry my first husband? I was living in fear and focusing on the what ifs. What if I don't have enough money? What if I move further away from my familiar surroundings and family and hate living there? What if I can't get as good a job as I have now at the bank? What if Jimmy procrastinates and we never end up getting married?

When I think about how many years of my life I wasted questioning the future instead of living in the moment, it makes me SO glad that I worked my way out of that habit.

I learned the hard way that most of those what if's will never happen and we can bring undesired things to us because we all possess powerful abilities to create even more misery in our lives whether we realize it or not. The future is not written yet and I don't want to live there or manifest fear based things into my reality.

Learning to have faith, even when the outcome isn't obvious has changed my life in so many positive ways and I am happier and healthier because of it.

Lesson Five – Forgive

Forgiveness is a really big one. In face, I feel forgiveness is so important that I plan to write a book on forgiveness someday. I have met some powerful forgivers, and I am inspired by them and by how practicing forgiveness has changed their lives and the lives of others. Just remember, we do not forgive to release others from assuming responsibility, we forgive in order to release the negative, destructive energy from our bodies that hanging on to anger and regret creates.

Holding onto the past and not forgiving can create the same detrimental effects as negative self talk, self loathing and guilt. These behaviors bring your vibration down to the lowest points and eventually can make you physically ill.

Guilt and not forgiving are usually based on living in the past, and when we live in the past we live a life of regrets with all of the woulda, shoulda, coulda's. One of the greatest joys of my life was marrying Jimmy and if I would not have forgiven myself for all of those bad decisions that caused me to be married to other people for over decades, for not giving him the chance to work things out before I married my first husband, for struggling with the decision to be with him at last – I could have let myself get mired in the mud of guilt and regret and blame. And, had Jimmy not forgiven me for all of the things that could have kept us apart, our lives would be very different now.

Thankfully, we both learned to just let it go. You can do the same – and the sooner the better. Get some good books, meditate, ask God and his Angels to help you and make a promise to your new self that you will not live in the past.

Lesson Six – Be Grateful

Being grateful means appreciating the things that happen in our daily lives and focusing on what we have instead of what we lack. Being grateful means seeing the glass as half full instead of half empty. It also means trusting that everything happens for a reason and being thankful for life's challenges for they are our best teachers. Being grateful also means taking the time to regularly thank our Angels and other people for the support and assistance they provide.

I learned over time to be grateful for all of the lessons I asked to learn before coming into this life. I will often connect with my Angels and tell them that I am done with a certain lesson in this lifetime, and ask them to send me signs that this lesson is over. We must feel gratitude in our hearts in order to find a place of peace.

One of the greatest things about gratitude is that we often identify things to be grateful for when we compare them to other experiences that weren't so positive. I am so grateful for my life today because I can compare the joy of being with my true soul partner as opposed to being married to people with whom I wasn't in alignment. I am grateful for my teachers and remember a time when I was struggling to find wisdom. I am grateful for my work as a healer and for the metaphysical gifts that have been revealed to me so that I can be even more effective. The list of things for which I am grateful goes on and on.

When we are experiencing those really terrible challenges, just believing that they are happening to teach us lessons we need to fulfill our purpose can be very helpful. Eventually, by practicing some of the lessons I am sharing here, you will find your way to happiness, peace and a sincere perspective of gratitude.

Lesson Seven – Practice Compassion

What I mean by practicing compassion is that we, or at least many of us, compare ourselves and our lives to others and what we perceive as their perfect life and we desire what others appear to have. We do this because we are not satisfied and always searching for those things we think will make us happy. And, often, we believe in society's definition of success and think that we need to have a certain body type or a certain amount of money or a certain amount of children or a certain type of job in order to be a good person.

Compassion comes from understanding others and from seeing them as souls who have much in common with each other because they are children of the Divine and because they all search and struggle. One of the ways we can also show compassion is through generosity.

I am a giver. It just makes me feel good to be able to give with no expectations of something in return. I have always given and now I give with blessings and with my heart in anticipation that it will ease another's life or help in some way. I give with no strings attached. I do not and will never know if that homeless guy on the street used that five bucks for food or if he bought a bottle of wine with it. I don't even think about it because giving makes me feel good.

I do not always give monetary things. Many times, I give a free or discounted healing session or a small crystal or something I have made like a Sacred Spaces Pillowcase or a smile or compliment. It is not what we give that is important - it is how we give and our intentions around giving.

Giving helps us to feel better about ourselves and takes the focus away from *our* problems and issues and replaces those with the energy of kindness and compassion. The more we give, the more we will receive.

Giving can heal our physical illnesses, also. I recommend you read "29 Gifts" by Cami Walker. Trust me on this one. I repeat, giving can heal on many levels. Compassion for others is one of the highest vibrations on the planet.

Become a mindful giver if you are not currently doing this. Compassion and kindness can change our lives and can change the world. Practice them at every opportunity.

Lesson Eight – Believe in Miracles

We have spoken quite a bit about Divine timing and Divine messages and miracles. One of the things I discovered when Dad had his NDE was that not everything in life is logical and explainable. When Jimmy and I found each other again and were able to marry and be together, I knew that miracles beyond our wildest imagination
really do happen. Magic and miracles abound, and all we need to do is to be open to them.

Here is how you can open yourself up to miracles:

- *Ask for MAGIC to appear in your life each day before your feet hit the ground*

- *Be open to the MIRACLES that happen when you communicate with Your Angels and with the Divine*
- *Set your INTENTION through meditation and prayer*
- *Ask for the SIGNS and don't worry about them*
- *Act upon what you RECEIVE by expressing gratitude and taking positive action (baby steps are fine)*
- *In all things practice Love, Compassion, Patience, Gratitude and Kindness*

Lesson Nine – Get to Know Your Angels

This book is called The Angel's Orchestra because Angels have been a pivotal influence in my life since I was a child. I first became aware of my intuitive abilities when I had predictive dreams.

The miracle of my dad's Near Death Experience led me to begin studying spirituality and the metaphysical and created a foundation of knowledge on which I was able to build as a healer.

I began working with Angels more seriously and with intention after attending Charles Virtue's workshop and this single event placed me firmly on the path to fulfilling my purpose as a teacher and a healer.

Asking my Angels to bring me signs to lead me in my journey resulted in me being married to my soul partner and living a life based on love and joy. Asking for signs also led me to workshops that changed my life and helped me expand my mission of service.

Studying to develop my intuition and doing readings at fairs have taught me to appreciate and value my intuitive gifts. I have also been inspired to study and work as an energy healer to help others recover and strengthen their physical health; to provide intuitive guidance to others to help them identify their life purposes and move forward, to lead past life regressions to assist others in knowing the specifics of their soul's journeys and to inform their progress in this lifetime; and to work with the Angels to share messages from the departed to help others heal in their grieving journeys.

The Angel's Orchestra is full of generous, powerful, loving, compassionate Angels who are ready and willing and able to help us all, each and every day and we only need to do two simple things – ask and believe.

The Angel's Orchestra

Chapter 17

Conclusion

As we approach the end of this path, we realize that it is not an ending, but rather a beginning. We can choose to embrace the miracles and move forward in harmony with our Angels.

We have come to the end of this little book and I feel in many ways I have only scratched the surface of what I wanted to share with you when I began writing it a few years ago.

I have, indeed, continued to learn and evolve, and in reading this book, you have chosen to do the same.

I have always considered myself to be open and curious. I love to study and read. I am not an expert, but I know a little about a lot of subjects. I am a true

Gemini. I feel like there are so many books - and so little time. Audio books are my new friends.

I consider myself a facilitator and enjoy referring people who come to me to the experts I know or to the books I have read. There is a list of many of these books at the end of this one.

The world is so full of information. We live in an age of information overload. Search and you will find answers to your questions. Ask and you will receive.

I cannot explain why the miracles in my life have happened to me. I know I am not alone. I know there are others out there who are experiencing these mystical things and many more who would love to have some clear guidance in their lives.

I also know that with intention we all have the ability to connect with our Angels and higher selves and that this can lead us to that place where we can experience the miracles we so desire. I know it is possible because it happened to me. If it can happen to me it can happen to any one of you. Ask and Open your Eyes. Be as a child, open and receptive.

Here are a few things to think about before you put this book back on the shelf.

Connect each day with your Angels, guides and higher self. Ask them to give you signs. Tell them you are ready for them to be active in your life now.

Think about what your gifts are and take the steps necessary to use those gifts to help you and to help others.

Tell God and his Angels 'Thank You' often.

Love yourself and love others with no prejudice or judgment.

Be kind and generous in all things.

Live a compassionate and grateful life.

Forgive everything and let go of guilt.

Work to stay in a high vibrational energy.

Live in the present.

Develop your intuition.

Teach others if you are guided to do so.

Help others when you can.

Be open to miracles. Ask for them.

Watch your words for they are powerful, as powerful as your thoughts.

Write down what you want, voice what you want and connect and pray about what you want.

Pay attention because the Universe is always communicating with you.

Appreciate your life and what others do for you.

The Angel's Orchestra

> Do not allow your fears to shape your life or others to project their fears and energy on you.
>
> Until we meet again I wish for you the blessings of peace and love and for God to send his messengers to your side so you can live a life of no regrets.
>
> God Bless

Appendix

To make things easier for you, I've decided to include some information about how to read Tarot cards, the Green Tara mantra, and my recommended book list here in the Appendix.

How to Read Cards of any Kind

As with all my beliefs and teachings, when it comes to reading Angel, Tarot or oracle cards, I invite you to take what resonates with you and leave the rest on the table. This is my work and what I do and one of the things I teach. When you are guided to do this work, by doing intuitive and card readings for others, always remember that intuition is a gift not to be taken lightly. Do not abuse your gifts.

Here are the most important things to know before you begin:

- When reading for others, ask your angels to provide information for their highest good.

- Intuition can be developed with practice and desire.

- We are all different and our gifts are as varied as our personalities.

- We are happiest when we are helping others in some way, shape, or form.

- We are all here to help one another heal.

- As we help others heal, we also heal ourselves.

First of all, there is nothing wicked, woo-woo or magic about any of the tools of Divinity that people have used for thousands of years. Tarot cards are simply instruments that connect us spiritually to a deeper, more expansive part of ourselves. This is the part of us that knows there are no limits. These sacred tools, and there are many, very simply stated, connect us to our source and our spiritual helpers aka Angels, guides and our higher selves. We are so much more than we can even imagine ourselves to be.

If you have the desire to read cards and you follow these steps, you will be reading Tarot and oracle cards for yourself and for others in no time at all.

Purchase the deck that you are most drawn to, use kinesiology; hold the deck in your dominant hand. Extend your opposite arm out to the side of you so that it is parallel to the ground. Ask another person to press down on your hand that is not holding the card deck. If your hand holds firm and does not push down easily, then this deck is in alignment with your energy. If your hand can be easily pushed toward the ground, choose another deck and repeat the process. Once you have found your deck, Clear, Sanctify and infuse your energy on the cards. Clear by knocking 3 times on the deck as you hold it in your non-dominant hand, say a prayer of gratitude calling in your Angels, Guides and higher self to help you receive and give the best information possible, touch each card to infuse your energy and your intention into the cards. Set your intention that the messages that come to you through this deck are from the highest sources of wisdom and that they provide messages for the highest good for you and the person for whom you are reading.

Remember to connect with the energy of the person you are reading for. This is accomplished in several different ways, by looking into their eyes, by them saying their name and repeating it 3 times, by shuffling the cards as the client is asking their question or giving their name, by touching their hand, by their touching the tarot cards you will be using as you look into their eyes, by asking your angels and guides to connect with theirs. Try throwing an energy ball into their heart and expanding that energy to encompass you. Try feeling their heart energetically.

Find what works best for you, because we are all different and our guides and Angels work with us in different ways. Ask them to guide you. Ask them to 'Be There.' Find what works for you and remember it may be different for each person who sits in front of you. Some clients will be easy to connect with while others more difficult. Energy is energy. Some are wide open and others shut off. You will begin to just know things about the person sitting in front of you the moment they sit down as your sensitivity and your gifts grow. Accept it.

Once you lay down the cards, pay attention to what the card is telling you. A card can repeat the same message to you many times, reading after reading, but sometimes it will give you a different meaning than what you have grown accustomed to. Yes, it is OK to learn the traditional meanings of the cards, but more often than not when you use a deck over and over it will begin to talk to you. Touch the cards.

Look at the pictures. How do they make you feel? What is the first thing your eyes are drawn to? Do you hear anything, feel anything, sense anything or just simply know something? What is being activated in your soul when you look at or touch that card? What are you feeling and where? Do you get the energy bumps? If so, PAY ATTENTION.

Reading the Picture on the Card

I am going to share with you the easiest, most intuitive way to read a Tarot or oracle card of any type. This technique is even better than memorizing the complex meanings of cards found in books. While those books are helpful, I believe that jumping in and getting started is the best way to learn tarot as we are all intuitive and can do this work if we so desire with pure intention.

Did you know that the earliest tarot cards were created in the 1400's when most people could not read and one of the most effective ways to convey deep spiritual lessons and important sacred texts was through the use of pictures?

Tarot cards are imbued with rich symbolism and imagery because they were once used in various religious and spiritual circles. That is the reason they were created. (We all know that the church came in and banned the use of many Gnostic texts' sacred knowledge and tools in order to gain more control of the people.) This is why so many people fear using their intuitive and healing gifts. Obviously, I am not one of them!

Knowing the cards were created for the message in their imagery, how do you think the easiest way to read cards is? Yep, "Read the picture" or "The answer is in the picture." You must connect with the picture in order to receive the message. What is going on in the picture? Are there numbers? What is the symbolism? Colors? Energy of the card? What is moving or what is the activity you are drawn to in the card? How does the picture make you feel? What part of your body do you feel that energy in? When you touch the card, do you see or hear anything or simply know something? Close your eyes. Do you see anything? It is helpful to know some basic symbolism and numerology, but not even necessary. YOU get to interpret the picture on the card. You get to turn on your intuition through the images. I believe the messages will come to you if you simply have a desire to do this work and take the steps through your fears.

Ask your Angels and Guides to be with you, they are the ones who will be feeding you amazing information if you will ask and then be receptive. The more you trust them, the more they will provide.

Each card tells a story and that story can be told in many varied ways. What is your eye drawn to? What is the basic symbolism? More importantly, What does that symbol mean to you? How do you react to where your eye has landed? Sometimes the two do not match. Always go with your intuition and ask, "What does this mean?"

God and the Angels will often bring people to you who have experienced similar things in their own lives. Like attracts like. Remember this.

What attracts your attention? Gaze at the cards again and see if something more grabs your eye or if one card in the 'lay' pulls at you emotionally. Touch that card. How do you feel, do you see or hear anything? Consciously make an effort to find something in the card that you did not find before. Ask the card what it is trying to tell you and it will tell you.

Breathe and drink plenty of water. Energy moves in your body through water and breath. Deep belly breath on 4 count, pause a second and 4 count, release. Do this about 10 times. Imagine an infinity symbol connecting your head and heart and your heart and solar plexus. Ground and protect your energy consciously and with intent by imaging yourself in a protective egg of white, pink or golden light which shields you from absorbing others' energies. Carry one of the protective stones in your pocket set with the same intention or a crystal bracelet.

OK, I am going to say something here that some of you may not like. There are some professionals who want Tarot to seem like it is super complicated and hard to learn. They charge huge amounts of money to teach people the traditional meaning of the cards. Do not fall into their traps. It is not necessary to take classes for years or even months to learn to read tarot or oracle cards. Many of these so-called experts want their students to remain in the fog of not being able to crack the code or master reading cards.

You do not need to study for years and you do not need to pay a lot of money to learn to read cards. It is not complex and there are no buried secrets you have to uncover. You do not need to feed their ego or their pocketbook. If you have the urge and desire to do this work, then it is inside you. Begin and ask for the right teacher to come to you. When the student is ready . . .

Here is the honest truth.

It helps to learn some of the traditional meanings of cards. It helps to learn card symbolism. And yes, it helps to learn something about numerology, as these are all things that are embedded in the cards and much more. Buy a good book. Take a little class, but do not get involved in studying for years and paying out huge sums of money because the world needs your light right now. If Reading cards pulls at your heart and you have a sincere desire to help others your Angels and Guides will be by your side every step of the way. The hardest part is trusting what you receive and just getting out of your comfort zone and doing it.

Tarot is not hard and you will get the most out of it if you keep it simple and ask your higher self, guides and angels to assist you. It is that simple.

The hardest part is stepping through your fears and voicing what you receive. I promise.

If you are new to Tarot, don't get caught up in other's need to make things more frightening than they need to be. All you really have to have is a pure desire to learn and a yearning to help others with the information you receive. God and his Angels and your guides will provide you with what you need.

I believe that the real purpose of Tarot or any spiritual device we use to assist others is very simple. We are either validating something that is going on in another's life or we are providing ideas and inspiration. Many times, the messages delivered by Angel Card readers validates that there are Angels around us, wanting to communicate and guide us.

Tarot often helps us shift another's perception, provide them with hope and help them to move forward when they are stuck. Just think, all we have to do is relay the information we receive. All we have to do is connect and ask for the message in the card. Most times our energy shifts also so be prepared as often, the messages we receive are also for us to pay attention to.

Always give the information you receive in a kind and gentle way. We, for the most part do not know what is going on in another's life. Always remember kindness is a free gift we can give every single day.

Always ask for more information before you end a reading. You may be surprised at what you receive at the end of the session.

Be prepared as sometimes passed over loved ones will step in. Yes it is real and can begin to happen when we learn to trust what we are receiving. Form a close relationship with your guides and ask them to only open that door when you are ready and to close it if you are not ready.

The Green Tara Mantra
OM TARE TUTTARE TURE SOHA

When you chant her potent mantra with intense feeling and devotion, the mantra is transformed into a powerful wish-fulfilling prayer.

(Translation in English)

Om O Tara! I entreat you, O Tara! O swift one! Hail

OR

"I prostrate to the Liberator, Mother of all the Victorious Ones."

OM (prounounced OHM) represents the speech, body, and mind qualities of all the Buddhas. OM has no conceptual meaning and is a most sacred sound representing the entire universe, past, present and future.

Tare (pronounced TAH-RAY) represents salvation from suffering and mundane dangers. The word is translated as "the Swift One."

Tuttare (pronounced TOO-TAH-RAY) represents the protection from all our fears and the deliverance into the spiritual path, in terms of individual salvation.

Ture (pronounced TOO-RAY) represents the fulfillment of our spiritual path. Meaning we want to develop all of the positive qualities and we want to purify all our negative ones.

Soha (pronounced SEW-HAH) means 'so be it,' 'may it be like that' or 'May a blessing rest on.'

Reciting the mantra—

OM TARE TUTTARE TURE SOHA

Take a breath and and recite the entire mantra above now that you know how to pronounce the words. Take a breath and recite again.

Next, breath into your heart (you do this by imagining your heart is taking the breath rather than your lungs). You should immediately feel the difference as your heart energy expands. I like to recite the mantra before I meditate. It relaxes me and I go into meditative states more deeply and more quickly.

I normally sit on my couch or a chair which supports my back to meditate but you can sit yoga style or any way that is comfortable for you. There are no rules.

It is a good idea to set your intention to connect with Green Tara if that is what you desire to do or you can simply chant the mantra while sending love and peace into the universe.

Benefits of Chanting the Green Tara Mantra

By chanting this powerful mantra with sincere motivation and feeling, it is believed that one will be able to invoke the blessings of Goddess Tara and request for her protection from danger and from fears. Additionally, the mantra can be used to overcome mental, physical, or emotional blockages as well as blockages in relationships.

It is believed that reciting the mantra daily can eliminate disease, fear, anxiety, suffering, disasters, troubles, and negative karma.

According to a Buddhist teacher Sangharakshita (founder of the Triratna Buddhist Community), a traditional explanation of the mantra is that the variations of her name represent three progressive stages of salvation.

The Angel's Orchestra

A List of Books and Other Things

As promised here is a list of books, authors, and workshops I recommend often to clients and students. This is not an inclusive list.

I am passionate about studying and reading and always adding to my knowledge. I hope you are too.

Many of these books have been written by personal friends of mine and mentioned throughout this book. I am blessed to have so many wonderful teachers and role models in my life and meeting them was no accident. Those books have an asterisk.

*James Patrick Lane: Improve your Being–Improve Your Life

*James Patrick Lane: Messages from an Enchanted Forrest

*Lane Robinson: Enlightened by Accident–The Awakening of a Psychic Medium

*Shelley Kaehr: Any of her books. Shelley is one of my personal mentors and gifted.

*PJ Spur: Navigating Grief with Grace

*Steve Spur: Crossroads

*Lillis Owen: Visions Of A Sacred Truth–An Akashic Journey

*LaRue Eppler and Vanessa Tabor Wesley: Your Essential Whisper

Brian Weiss: Any of his books, courses and conferences

Wayne Dyer: Any of his books, courses and conferences

Louise Hay: You Can Heal Your Life and any of her books or courses

Edgar Cayce: Any of his books

Robert Schwartz: Your Soul's Plan and any of his books

Annie Kagan: The Afterlife of Billy Fingers

James L Wilson: Adrenal Fatigue: The 21st Century Stress Syndrome

Neville Goddard: Any of his books. Neville opens us up to the power of using the gift of imagination.

Automated Writing: Any books around this subject.

Raymond Moody: Any of his books and books you are drawn to around Near death Experiences or NDE's.

Bronnie Ware: The Top Five Regrets of the Dying

Cami Walker: 29 Gifts

Gary Finley: Letting Go

Susan Carrell, RN, LPC: Escaping Toxic Guilt

Cheryl Richardson: Stand up for Your Life

Susanne Summers: Breakthrough

Masaru Emoto: Love Thyself

Janet Conner: Writing down Your soul

Judith Orloff: Any of her books-especially her teachings about Empaths

Sandy Grason: Journalution

Lois Guarino: Writing Your Authentic self

Piero Ferrucci: The Power of Kindness

Hay House Publishing: Any of their books, courses, conferences and related materials you are drawn to

Past Life Regressions: Any books around this subject you are drawn to.

Ley Lines: Ley Lines are fascinating to me. Search out material and study this topic if it resonates with you.

Dowsing: I am a dowser. Discover the power of dowsing and find out if you are gifted in the area.

For those interested in Reiki there is a wealth of information on the International Center of Reiki Training website where I am listed as one of the affiliate teachers. I teach in person in the DFW area. www.reiki.org is the ICRT's website.

The Angel's Orchestra

Dedication & Acknowledgements

This book is dedicated to my husband, James Patrick Lane. We have lived many lives together with many more to come. You are my better half, my heart, and my greatest teacher. I SEE you. You paved the way for this book and played a part in many of the stories found here.

This book is also dedicated to my two daughters, Kelly and Sharla. I know I do not resemble the Mother who raised you. You tell me this often. I am not that person. I am changed. I encourage you to grow and to learn your own truth, to dream the grandest dreams possible for your own lives and put those dreams into action. I love you always and eternally.

I would also like to acknowledge James Patrick Lane for his beautiful painting, Soul Solace and for the cover design of this book. I would also like to thank all of those who generously allowed me to share their stories, especially Charles Virtue, Sherry XXXX, PJ Spur, Steve Spur, and Lane Robinson. Thank you for being a part of my journey in this lifetime.

I would also like to thank my dear friend, Lane Robinson for editing this book. She worked with me to transform this second edition into a simpler, more elegant version of the original.

Last but not least, I dedicate this book to my teachers, my students, and my clients. *You know who you are.* You inspire me and I learn from you always. You are the reason this book of life experiences is here. For you all, my tribe, my family, my soul group, may the Angels of Heaven bless each one of you with God's Grace so you can experience your lives with your Orchestra of

Angels each and every day.

The Angel's Orchestra

About the Author

Rev. Patricia LaDale Lane, BMsc lives in Fort Worth, Texas USA with her husband James. She holds a Bachelors degree in Metaphysical Science from The University of Sedona.

Her ministry is a metaphysical one and her passion is teaching women to develop their intuitive gifts so they can heal themselves and overcome the fears in their lives. Patricia is an author, speaker, metaphysical teacher, Holy Fire Karuna Reiki® Master teacher, a Past Life Regressionist, Medium and Intuitive. She does sessions by phone and in person at holistic fairs in the Dallas-Fort Worth area.

Patricia lectures and teaches workshops based on her personal experiences and her book.

www.etsy.com/shop/sacredpillowcase

Patricia's website is sacredspacesbypatricia.com.

Connect with her on Facebook in The Angel's Orchestra group or send a friend request to join her personal page Patricia Ladale Lane.

The Angel's Orchestra

Made in the USA
Middletown, DE
21 August 2024